EVERYDAY BOUQUET

EVERYDAY BOUQUET

13-Digit ISBN: 978-1-64643-445-9
10-Digit ISBN: 1-64643-445-5

This book may be ordered by mail from the publisher. Please include $5.99 for postage and handling. Please support your local bookseller first!

Books published by Cider Mill Press Book Publishers are available at special discounts for bulk purchases in the United States by corporations, institutions, and other organizations. For more information, please contact the publisher.

Cider Mill Press Book Publishers
"Where good books are ready for press"
501 Nelson Place
Nashville, Tennessee 37214

cidermillpress.com

Typography: Adobe Text Pro, Futura PT, Scotch Display Condensed
Endpaper vectors used under official license from Shutterstock.com.

Printed in China

24 25 26 27 28 TYC 5 4 3 2 1
First Edition

EVERYDAY BOUQUET

52 BEAUTIFUL ARRANGEMENTS FOR EVERY SEASON

BY
ALEX VAUGHAN

PHOTOGRAPHY BY
NICOLA HARGER

CIDER MILL PRESS

BOOK
PUBLISHERS

CONTENTS

INTRODUCTION

In the tapestry of life, every season paints its own narrative, expresses its own emotion, reveals its own beauty. This book is an ode to those ever-changing seasons and the wondrous blooms and foliage they graciously bestow upon us. Each page unravels a tale of a week in the year, as we journey from the rejuvenating whispers of spring to the tranquil introspection of winter's end.

The art of floral arrangement goes beyond mere aesthetics; it's an intimate dance with nature, a song of reverence for the environment. *Everyday Bouquet* is anchored in the ethos of using seasonal blooms and foliage. This approach not only lends each arrangement its unique character but also harmonizes with a sustainable vision, significantly reducing the environmental footprint of the bouquet. Each flower, in its natural blooming cycle, brings with it an authenticity, a freshness that is irreplaceable.

But the charm of *Everyday Bouquet* doesn't end there. This book is a clarion call to every novice designer, every individual who has admired the daisies in their yard or the ivy creeping up a wall. There's magic lurking in every corner of your garden, every patch of wildflowers in front of your home. With a pinch of inspiration and a dash of creativity, the most unexpected elements can transform into stunning centerpieces. Your personal touch, combined with the guidance of this book, will unearth beauty in places you've always looked at, but perhaps never truly seen.

To bolster your journey, a section dedicated to arranging techniques awaits your exploration. Drawing from timeless traditions and contemporary innovations, these techniques serve as the foundation, the stepping stones, to craft your own unique floral narratives.

Everyday Bouquet is more than just a coffee-table adornment. It's an invitation—a call to immerse ourselves in nature's bounty, to foster a deeper connection with our environment, and to find joy and wonder in the petals and leaves that often go unnoticed.

May you find inspiration in these pages, not just for floral arrangements, but for embracing the beauty and rhythms of everyday life. As you craft your own arrangements, may you be reminded of nature's wonders, the art of presence, and the magic that exists in every bloom.

UNDERSTANDING FLORAL DESIGN PRINCIPLES

BALANCE

The concept of balance often evokes the image of a vintage scale, perfectly poised with equilibrium on both sides. Yet, the allure of an imbalanced scale, one side dipping while the other rises, has always captivated me. It breaks away from mundane symmetry and ventures into a realm of intriguing asymmetry. In the world of floral design, I encourage you to visualize this scale, not with the intent of achieving perfect balance, but to understand the relational dynamics between the elements. Every change on one side directly affects the other, creating a harmonious dance of contrast. Striking balance in floral artistry isn't about equal weight or matching heights; it's about creating visual harmony where every component complements one another. It's not always evident and can often be nuanced. For example, delicate tendrils reaching skyward can be counterbalanced by a dense cluster at the base, or perhaps by a mirroring swoop of similar tendrils extending diagonally. In your designs, seek a relationship between elements that, while not always symmetrical, results in a visually cohesive and compelling arrangement. Balance is first on the list of principles because it is the key to success. Almost everything else can be thought of in terms of balance when broken down into smaller points.

PROPORTION

Delving into the notion of proportion is like zooming in to the concept of balance and magnifying its influence on each distinct element of your arrangement. It's about ensuring every element fits and complements the others, both in size and significance. Take daffodils, for example: on their own, a single stem might appear too modest. But, when grouped together, they can create an impactful visual mass. This principle is evident in Week 3's arrangement (page 30). Every component, from the focal flower to the smallest accent, should have a clear and proportional relationship to the others. Your focal flower should always be proportionally more prominent, in either scale or repetition, than your accentuating elements.

SCALE

At its heart, scale is a yet another form of balance, where the size of materials should align harmoniously with the container and its intended space. Let's consider the vessel: it can serve as the muse for your composition or play a supporting role to a chosen flower or foliage. The word "materials" here encompasses both flowers and foliage. A dainty vessel, for instance, beckons for equally delicate materials—think flowers with petite heads or slender, twining tendrils. Conversely, if you're drawn to more substantial materials like grand monstera leaves or statuesque pampas grass, they call for a container with a presence to match.

Your arrangement's ultimate home is crucial in defining its scale. Take, for example, an expansive, round entry table in a foyer. It requires an arrangement whose scale resonates with the room's essence. Consider elements like an overhead light fixture, the height of the ceiling, and the room's overall ambiance, be it cavernous or cozy. These facets of the environment should inform and inspire the scale of your floral creation. Remember, every element has its part to play, and recognizing these relationships is key to mastering scale.

EMPHASIS OR FOCAL POINT

Just as every story has a main character, every floral arrangement needs a focal point. This is the star of the show, the element that immediately draws the eye. Often, it's a singular, standout bloom, but it can also be a distinct design element or shape within the arrangement. If you compare floral arranging to writing, your focal flower is your protagonist. Classic storytelling typically features one main protagonist. However, a clever and experienced writer could write a story with more than one protagonist—or a story where you're not quite sure who the real protagonist is—in a way that is intriguing rather than confusing. It's the same for floral design. Start simple, master the basics, and then try more complicated methods with time and experience behind you. I recommend starting out by making a single bloom the object of your focus. Think of it as building a cast around a main character in a play. Start with a clear protagonist in your arrangements. As you become more adept, you can experiment with multiple focal points or more subtle emphasis, but always ensure clarity and intention in your designs. The aim is to guide the viewer's eye, not to confuse it. Master the basics first, and with experience, you can introduce more complexity to your creations.

MOVEMENT AND DIMENSION

Floral arrangements come to life with the careful interplay of movement and dimension. While certain principles of floral design become second nature over time, these two elements require ongoing attention and refinement, no matter how seasoned the designer.

Dimension is relatively straightforward. Achieving it demands a game of push and pull: embed some flowers deeper, making them a background element, while drawing others to the foreground for prominence. Allow some stems to stretch out, reaching the edges of your arrangement, and let others stay close to the core. The interplay of light and shadow further accentuates dimension. Position some blooms to capture light, while others recede into softer, shaded areas.

Movement, on the other hand, is a more nuanced principle. It's not just about positioning your flowers to face forward or outward. To ensure movement, let your flowers adopt varied directions. For instance, in Week 41 (page 173), observe how many dahlias face inward, urging the viewer's eye to travel deeper into the arrangement. Movement can also be created by playing with the natural tendencies of your materials. Take the design from Week 5 (page 38): the crab apple branches curve upward, as if resisting gravity, while some of the fritillaria hang down, gracefully yielding to it. This duality creates a dynamic that makes the arrangement both compelling and balanced. The best advice I can give for movement is to have it, but keep it subtle.

CONTRAST

Contrast in floral design involves juxtaposing elements to accentuate their distinct qualities. When you've determined your arrangement's focal point, introduce elements that enhance its prominence and others that distinctly set against it. For instance, a voluminous peony can be highlighted with the delicate texture of astilbe, emphasizing the peony's lushness through contrast. Color, too, is a powerful tool for contrast. Consider the arrangement from Week 34 (page 146): the dark ninebark foliage sets a stark backdrop for the soft blush of the lisianthuses, making the latter pop. However, when playing with contrast, it's crucial to strike a balance. The sharp contrast in Week 34 works because of the lisianthuses' dark centers and their setting against a black vase. Absent these complementary elements, the contrast could be jarring rather than enhancing.

SPACE

Negative space in an arrangement can dramatically alter its overall ambiance. A compact design with minimal negative space may exude a sense of structure and formality. In contrast, a more open arrangement, generous with negative space, can evoke sensations of natural wilderness and spontaneous beauty. Thus, the strategic use of negative space becomes pivotal in floral design.

When incorporating negative space, intentionality is paramount. Unplanned or indiscriminate use of negative space may lead an arrangement to appear accidental and lacking design coherence. One must also be attentive to how stems are presented within the arrangement. Unlike in painting or drawing, in floral design, no flower can truly be suspended in thin air; stems serve as their grounding line. However, not all stems are aesthetic in their natural state. Avoid displaying stems that introduce jarring straight lines in an otherwise organic setup. Opt for stems with graceful curves or camouflage less appealing stems with lighter, textured elements.

Conversely, arrangements with scant negative space risk appearing flat and two-dimensional. For such designs, introducing dimension and movement is especially vital to breathing life into the composition.

COLOR

Mastering color theory, especially the nuances of complementary and analogous shades, is crucial for impactful floral arrangements. The deliberate use of color can establish harmony, introduce contrast, or emphasize particular elements, but gaining proficiency requires time and practice.

For those starting out in floral design, I advocate focusing on analogous color combinations—like purple and blue or pink and orange. These neighboring hues on the color wheel possess an innate compatibility. For instance, while orange and pink may seem distinct, their intermediate shades often blend seamlessly.

Often, a flower won't fit neatly into a single color category upon close inspection. Consider the Free Spirit rose. At a glance, it might be deemed orange. However, an in-depth examination reveals undertones of peach, hints of pink, and even subtle yellow streaks, all enriching its primary orange hue. Recognizing these nuances, such as how the gentle pink at the tips of a Free Spirit rose can resonate with the pink of a fuzzy eucalyptus flower, introduces you to the concept of "color bridges." These bridges, while more evident when working with analogous colors, are invaluable tools in tempering stark contrasts between entirely different shades. The composition from Week 1 (page 22) exemplifies this technique in action.

REPETITION

Repetition, the act of echoing specific elements like blooms, colors, or textures, plays an essential role in achieving cohesiveness and rhythm in floral arrangements. Rarely can a singular flower stand alone in a design without detracting from the overall aesthetic. We, as humans, are naturally drawn to patterns; they bring comfort and familiarity. Weaving repeated elements throughout an arrangement invites the eye to dance across the composition, bringing a sense of pleasure and satisfaction. The artistry lies in crafting a design where the repetition feels natural and unforced, creating subtle patterns that may not be immediately apparent but contribute to the arrangement's overall allure.

VARIETY

Variety brings a zest to floral design, serving as the antidote to monotony and infusing creativity and innovation into arrangements. Diversity of ideas and materials offers endless opportunities for experimentation and delight. While sourcing from local growers and wholesalers is a tried-and-true method, the real adventure begins when one steps outside the traditional avenues. As highlighted in this book, the charm often lies in the unexpected: the commonplace petunia reinvented in a fresh design, houseplant cuttings given new life, or even fruits and vegetables playing the role of the unexpected star in an arrangement. With an open mind, every corner of the world—from gardens to grocery stores—transforms into a treasure trove of potential design elements. However, a word of caution: when venturing into foraging or backyard harvests, ensure you pick during cooler parts of the day, and give the floras some time to rest and hydrate before using them to help prevent your cuttings from "crashing."

COMMONLY USED TOOLS AND MECHANICS

STRAIGHT WIRE: A thin and malleable wire used for supporting or extending the stems of flowers. It comes in a few gauges. I find the 20 gauge to be the most useful across the board.

CHICKEN WIRE: A flexible mesh made of wire. It's used to create a supportive structure inside a vase or container, helping flowers stay in place.

KNIFE: Used to cut flower stems at an angle. This helps the flowers absorb more water and nutrients from the vase. It takes time and practice to be comfortable using a knife, but in the end it's much faster and better for the longevity of the stems.

SNIPS: Small scissors with sharp blades used for cutting thin stems and leaves. My favorite are from the ARS brand. You'll often find more aesthetically pleasing floral snips marketed to those interested in floral design. While these are quite pretty, they are typically expensive, and I find them to be less practical than the ARS brand.

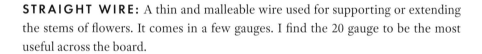

CLIPPERS: A heavier tool designed for cutting through thicker stems or branches. Again, I'm partial to the ARS brand, specifically the curved blade clippers. When dealing with very thick stems, it's also nice to have a ratcheting pair of clippers.

MÂCHÉ VASE LINER: A biodegradable liner for vases. It prevents any water leakage when you're using vessels meant to be for potted plants, which either have a hole or are water permeable. These liners can also add an extra layer of protection between the vase and whatever mechanics you might be using, such as chicken wire or foam.

GREEN OASIS TAPE: A waterproof tape used to secure floral foam to the base of a container or to bind together stems. This tape is only "waterproof" if you use it on a dry surface. It will absolutely never stick if water touches it before being stuck down. So be sure you use it dry and then add water, or wipe the surface you wish it to stick to thoroughly first.

VASE TAPE: A clear tape, typically ¼", used to create a grid on the opening of a vase. This helps hold flowers in place and provides structure to the arrangement.

FLORAL FOAM: A spongelike material that retains water. It's used as a base in many floral arrangements, allowing flowers to stay hydrated while also providing support. In addition to traditionally used floral foams, there are now many alternatives that do not contain any plastics or that claim to be more environmentally friendly in one way or another.

FLORAL FROG: A heavy, often metal object with spikes or holes. It's placed at the bottom of a vase to hold flower stems in place. Floral frogs are reusable and therefore considered to be more environmentally friendly than floral foam. Keep in mind when using these that the shape of your arrangement will likely not last beyond a day, as the integrity of the stems will eventually cave where they've been stabbed into the spikes.

WATER PICKS: Small plastic tubes filled with water and capped with a lid. They're used to keep individual stems of flowers hydrated, especially when there is a risk of the stems being too short to reach into the vase to the water source.

Nature moves in cycles, and spring heralds the rebirth of life. It seemed only fitting to commence our journey in this season, meandering through summer and autumn, and culminating in the serene embrace of winter. Consider this book a source of inspiration rather than a step-by-step guide. Dive into each week's segment, soaking up design insights and tips to enrich your floral endeavors. Remember, this isn't a recipe book. Embrace the ideas, let the imagery guide you, but don't feel bound to replicate each arrangement exactly. While I've named specific flower varieties to broaden your floral horizons, I urge you not to obsess over mimicking the precise compositions. The essence of each week's narrative transcends the flowers depicted, adaptable to a myriad of blooms. Ultimately, my hope is to illuminate the path for you to discover the ideal blossoms for your creations, harmonizing with your space, season, container, and individual flair.

WEEK 1

Although there is a singular day marked as the "first day" of each season, nature, in reality, has no use for exact parameters. Whenever spring decides to slide in, there are telltale signs of her impending arrival. The hellebore, often referred to as the "Lenten rose," begins to bloom when all other flowers are still deciding whether it's safe to erupt. For this reason, she is often either the star or a supporting cast member in early spring arrangements.

Large, orange parrot tulips command immediate notice, their vivid hue exuding warmth and energy. These majestic flowers stand tall and proud, their blossoms unfurling with confidence, adding a sense of grandeur to the arrangement and serving as the feature flower of this composition. When looking closely at these petals, you can see brushstrokes of pink amidst the orange.

Complementing the fiery tulips are taupe roses. Their delicate petals create a soft contrast against the vibrant orange, lending a sense of balance and refinement to the overall aesthetic. Notice how there is a touch of orange in the very center of the rose, and pink on the outer petals. While these two feature flowers could at first seem contrary to each other, looking at both more carefully will reveal that the tulip is not just orange, nor is the rose just taupe.

Purplish-pink hellebores bring a subtle yet enchanting element to the arrangement by helping to bridge the elements of the two feature flowers. The hellebores' unique coloration adds depth and intrigue and highlights the tones that the roses and tulips have in common. The hellebores, with their intricate blooms, draw the viewer's gaze in, inviting closer examination and appreciation for their delicate beauty.

In addition to bridging the colors of the tulips and roses, the purple *Astrantia* and deep-pink butterfly ranunculus introduce additional layers of texture to the ensemble. The purple *Astrantia*, with its star-shaped blooms, adds a touch of whimsy, while the deep-pink butterfly ranunculus contributes a sense of playfulness and romance. These flowers intermingle harmoniously, creating a dynamic visual interplay.

The choice of the glass footed vase adds an element of transparency and elegance. It allows the viewer to appreciate the intricate layers and details of the flowers while providing a delicate foundation for their vibrant display. The arrangement shape exudes a sense of opulence and natural beauty by extending out of the vase in an exaggerated way. Together, these blossoms overflow from the glass vase, spilling over with abundance and vitality.

WEEK 2

The vessel, a modern, green, footed bowl, sets the stage with its sophisticated simplicity. The bowl comes from the MoMA's Raawii collection, which was inspired by the still lifes of the Dutch modernist Vilhelm Lundstrøm. Low and wide, it allows the arrangement to stretch horizontally, creating a panoramic vista and, as a result, giving it an intimate and inviting presence.

At the forefront of this ensemble are the white tulips, each petal kissed with purple brushstroke patterns. These markings seem like they could have been painted by an artist's hand, perfectly imperfect. The tulips lend a softness, their white and purple hues emanating a sense of purity and serenity. They're not mere flowers; they're a poetic expression, reaching out to the viewer with elegance and grace.

The picotee ranunculus, with their purple striping, work alongside the tulips to further illustrate the painterly quality of the arrangement. These remarkable flowers, with their intricate petals and unique coloring, interact with the rest of the ensemble in a delicate dance. Their whimsical appearance adds another layer of complexity, acting as a gentle echo to the purple motifs found in the other components.

The green-and-purple lady slipper orchids add an exotic flair, their unusual shape and vibrant colors acting as a captivating counterpoint to the tulips' simplicity. These orchids, almost otherworldly in their beauty, present a sculptural element, each one a study in perfection and complexity. They are the wild heart of the bouquet, a splash of daring to augment this modern, artistic arrangement.

Complementing these stars of the show are the strands of purple heather. They weave through the bouquet like gentle whispers, their tiny blossoms adding texture and depth. The heather's subtle movement guides the eye, providing a rhythmic flow that connects each element and invites closer inspection.

Together, these floral components converge in a symphony of color, form, and emotion. The modernity of the green footed bowl juxtaposed with the timeless charm of the flowers creates an arrangement that's not just a visual feast, but an exploration into the artful nature of floral design. It invites the onlooker to pause and reflect, to discover the beauty in details, and to find joy in the magical interplay of nature and the human hand.

WEEK 3

There is no flower more associated with the early days of spring than the cheerful yellow daffodil. In the South, the tips of their leaves emerge from the ground before the spring solstice has passed, promising that winter will end and everything will soon be green again. However, these lovely daffodils are so eager to bloom that the first few to blossom often get nipped by a late frost or two. Fortunately, they've evolved a papery sheath that protects the blooms as their stems grow taller. Only when the flowers reach their final height do they break free from their protective sheaths and open up. Before arranging them, I like to clean the daffodils by carefully removing the dried-up sheaths, as they are no longer necessary and can distract from the beauty of the blooms.

For this arrangement, I've chosen to use a delicate, cup-shaped glass vase with a tape grid. The shape is intended to create a feeling of lush overabundance, flowing out to triple the width of the vessel itself. Allowing the dainty, thin stems of these flowers to be visible through the glass accentuates the sensation of overabundance, as if the arrangement defies gravity.

In most arrangements, I seek to have flowers of varying head sizes and highlight one flower (usually the largest) as the main center of focus—the "feature flower."

However, to emphasize the cuteness and delicateness of these early spring flowers, I decided to keep them all relatively similar in size. The combination of these similarly sized, ruffled blooms creates an almost frothy display of playfulness and exquisite elegance. The yellow butterfly ranunculus mirrors the deepest yellow tones from the center of the daffodil throats, and the white sweet peas break up the yellow, allowing each flower to be seen and appreciated on its own and as a part of the whole. Notice how a few smaller blooms poke out a bit farther from the rest, disrupting the creation of a perfect mushroom shape that would make the arrangement feel too stiff and unnatural.

WEEK 4

In nature's palette, blue is a rare gem, sought-after by flower enthusiasts for generations. While true blue flowers remain scarce, sometimes the limitation is the inspiration, and that was certainly true for this arrangement. A search for blue arrangements on Pinterest yielded a lot of painted and dyed flowers, flowers that were more purple than blue, white arrangements with blue accents, and a whole lot of delphinium and hydrangea. I was inspired to create something in contrast to all of that, with deep sapphire tones spanning from shades of blue to soft periwinkle hues. Instead of the usual painted or purple-tinted imitations, we celebrate the true essence of blue with a delightful assortment of anemones, hyacinths, delphiniums, gentians, and sweet peas.

To house these stunning blossoms, I opted for a low, elegant, chinoiserie-style ceramic bowl, perfectly complementing the short stems of our blue stars. I used a ball of chicken wire and chose to mound it up higher than the bowl to help give the arrangement extra stability, since the stems of hyacinths are soft and tend to bend under the weight of their blooms. Using that bowing of hyacinth stems to add movement to the arrangement, I allowed them to swing down below the lip of the bowl, nearly touching the table on one side, while the delphinium stretched upward on the opposite side, creating asymmetrical balance.

Amidst the blue blooms, there are lighter blue sweet peas, providing a subtle contrast and adding a touch of delicacy to the overall composition. The sweet peas, with their softer hue, introduce a gentle and graceful element to the arrangement and add brilliance by creating contrast against the deep blue tones. The dark navy of the anemone centers creates further depth.

This early-spring arrangement is an embodiment of sophistication and timeless beauty. Embrace the magic of this rare color, where limitations themselves become a source of inspiration.

WEEK 5

In nature's unending dance of change and renewal, the transition between seasons gives birth to a canvas of color and form, of structure and wild spontaneity. The ceramic footed urn chosen for this week's arrangement possesses an ageless charm, reminiscent of ancient times when art and nature flowed seamlessly together. Utilizing the chicken wire as an architectural backbone allows the flowers to cascade, rise, and occupy their space in a manner that's both structured and organic. You want just enough chicken wire to create at least a couple of layers for your stems to balance on, but not so much that you can't get your thicker branches through. Use floral tape in an X shape across the top to keep the chicken wire from popping out.

Rising majestically, the blooming crab apple branches reach out, their blossoms like soft pink stars against the twilight sky of ranunculus. They introduce a wild element, reminiscent of orchards in full spring bloom, of the delicate balance between man's touch and nature's own artistic flair. When using woody branches such as those of this blooming crab apple, you want to start with them first to create your frame. Always remember to split woody stems up the middle or shave off the outer bark so the branch can drink adequately.

These branches, with their organic arches and splay of blossoms, create an airy canopy, allowing a delicate play of shadow and light. As always, the goal when designing is balance—not necessarily symmetry.

Boldly stepping into the spotlight are the bright-pink Charlotte ranunculus. These blossoms, with their layered petals, are like nature's intricate origami—each layer revealing a depth of color and delicacy. They are the heartbeats of this arrangement, pulsating with vibrancy and passion.

Acting as a complement, yet not to be overshadowed, the salmon ranunculus introduce a softer hue. They weave throughout the arrangement, their tones acting like a gentle sunrise, a morning blush. They converse harmoniously with their brighter counterparts, painting a narrative of color interplay that sings of spring's warmth.

Adding to the ensemble's complexity are the *Fritillaria persica*. Their bell-shaped blooms, cascading downward in a gradient of purple and green, add a touch of mystique. These flowers, with their unusual form, bridge the divide between the softness of the ranunculus and the bold structure of the crab apple branches.

The entirety of this composition, with its radiant color palette and diverse textures, is a testimony to nature's endless ability to surprise and enchant. Here, in a footed urn, we find a microcosm of spring's promise—a blend of elegance, vitality, and the ever-present whisper of rebirth.

WEEK 6

Every once in a while, the essence of a warm, sun-kissed afternoon finds itself encapsulated in a singular floral composition, and this week, such an arrangement is our muse. Housed in a ribbed terra-cotta pot, there's an inherent earthiness in this display, a nod to the rustic simplicity of nature's embrace. The flared opening of the vessel beckons the blooms outward, inviting them to dance in a gentle sway, reminiscent of flowers in the wild, basking under the sun.

Acting as the foundational structure, acacia branches—or the affectionately termed mimosa flower—sprawl with an elegant abandon. Their fluffy yellow blossoms bring to mind rolling spring hills at dawn, painting the base with a hue of warmth and promise. Their delicate, fernlike leaves add a feathery texture, a perfect juxtaposition against the bolder blooms that sit atop them. These gorgeous branches are a super-early sign of spring, usually blooming in late February through March, and make for a great base for many arrangements. They can also easily become a magical display on their own.

The white Iceland poppies rise like the morning sun, their large, paper-thin petals seeming to flutter with the softest breeze. With bright-yellow centers that mirror the yellow of the mimosa flowers, they carry an ethereal

quality, as if they've been painted onto this canvas with the gentle strokes of an artist's brush. These poppies, with their fleeting life spans, remind us of the transient beauty of the present moment.

Mingling with these poppies are the large peach parrot tulips. Their ruffled petals, streaked with deeper hues, emulate the very essence of a twilight sky. Their curvaceous form and gradient of color provide a depth and drama, a whisper of passion amidst the serene calmness of the other blooms.

Woven through this tapestry are the delicate white sweet peas. Their dainty, fluffy petals embrace the other flowers, acting as a gentle binding thread. These blossoms, simple yet profound, bring forth an air of innocence and purity, harmonizing with the more assertive presence of the poppies and tulips.

The entire composition spills out in overabundance, gently caressing the table it rests on. The upper tip of the arrangement climbs skyward to balance out the spill of the flowers along the edges.

Collectively, this ensemble celebrates the symphony of early summer afternoons long before summer has arrived, a moment in time when light, color, and texture converge to create a masterpiece. The terra-cotta pot, with its earthy countenance, grounds this flight of fancy, ensuring that while the spirit soars amidst the flowers, the roots remain deeply connected to the Earth's embrace.

WEEK 7

As we delve into the heart of this season, nature seems to have whispered a sonnet of serenity, painting a dreamscape in the gentlest shades of violet. This week's arrangement is a symphony of purple, each note played in a hue that ranges from deep lavender to a muted, almost gray shade, evoking an atmosphere of calm introspection.

Cradling this serene orchestra is a bell-shaped footed pot, sculpted from rough stone. Its texture, unpolished and beautifully raw, acts as the grounding element in this ethereal presentation, the juxtaposition reminding us of nature's duality: the rough and the refined, the wild and the cultivated.

The purple delphiniums, with their tall spires that reach gracefully toward the heavens, stand as vigilant sentinels. Each tiny blossom captures the grandeur of nature in its delicate form. While delphiniums often arrive in stick-straight postures, there are those serendipitous moments when you encounter ones that naturally curl and twist. When blessed with such unique specimens, it becomes an imperative to showcase them without any distractions. These delphiniums craft a dramatic backdrop, and rather than forming a uniform spray across the rear, they peak more prominently on the arrangement's left side. This asymmetry is counterbalanced by the cascading blooms on the right, ensuring that all elements hold their own on this botanical stage.

The Westminster Abbey garden roses, a muted shade of lavender, seem to have absorbed the twilight itself. Their intricate petals unfurl in quiet elegance, each layer whispering tales of ancient gardens and moonlit walks. Their size, when they are kept low in the arrangement, creates weight and a rest for the eye in a sea of texture. Equally captivating are the lavender spray roses. Smaller, yet no less significant, they inject a soft, dreamy romance into the scene and balance the purple of the delphinium with the almost imperceptible violet of the garden roses.

Complementing these roses, the hellebores—those beloved harbingers of early spring—offer their cup-shaped blooms, their coloration varying from one to the next, creating a subtle tapestry of purples. The statice sinuata-blush introduces a texture reminiscent of delicate lace, its tiny blossoms creating a misty veil amidst the bolder blooms.

Interspersed are sprigs of lilac, their clusters of fragrant flowers infusing the arrangement with an intoxicating aroma, a scent that seems to carry with it the promise of warmer days. The sterling range, with its silvery hue, reflects the light, adding a touch of luminosity, a soft glow that enhances the overall ethereal quality.

This composition is more than just a floral arrangement; it's a meditation in lavender, a visual lullaby that beckons the onlooker to pause, to breathe, and to find solace in the gentle embrace of nature's hues. It is a celebration of the quiet moments, the soft transitions, and the beauty that lies in the muted shades of life.

WEEK 8

I t's truly beginning to warm up now; the promise of summer is just beyond the horizon. Housed in a clay footed compote, this floral ensemble elegantly marries rustic charm with a delicate dance of hues and textures. The shallow nature of this compote necessitates the use of floral foam or your favorite eco-friendly alternative (but avoid using a frog for this one, as the stems of some of these flowers won't lend themselves well to it).

Dominating the ensemble with their lavish display are the large white clematis. Their pristine petals extend outward with a graceful boldness, but it's not just their blooms that enchant—the inclusion of their verdant greenery adds an intricate depth, reminding one of the clematis's wild origins and the way they can spread over and through the garden when not trained and secured onto a structure.

Nestled amongst the clematis are the Iceland poppies, in all their varying shades of peach. These poppies, delicate yet vibrant, bring forth an essence of whimsy and fleeting beauty. Their paper-thin petals seem to flutter even in the stillness, casting fleeting shadows and catching the light in a soft, warm embrace. The singular poppy bobbing above the rest on the right side directly balances the low-slung clematis that seems to be making a break for it off to the left.

Joining this symphony are the bold peachy-orange tulips, which, with their curved and confident petals,

infuse a splash of warmth and charisma. Their curvaceous blooms, with hues reminiscent of a summer sunset, arch gently, lending a sense of movement and rhythm to the composition. In good floral design, stems are rarely displayed in favor of the obvious prize of the head of a flower. However, the stem of the tulip is just as much a part of her sophistication as the flower itself, and artfully displaying the curve of the stems will add to the charm of an arrangement. Their elegance is undeniable, their presence undeniable. A fact about tulips that many don't realize is that their stems continue to lengthen, in search of the sun, even after being cut. So be careful when designing with tulips that you account for that growth; otherwise, the next day you'll have tulip tentacles sticking out all over the place, and the balance of your elegant arrangement will be entirely off. You can also remove, trim, and replace tulips as they age to help with this issue.

Finally, the peach ranunculus and Julianne spray roses punctuate the arrangement with their tightly layered blossoms. Each one is like a secret waiting to be unfurled, adding texture and a touch of romance. Their soft hue mirrors that of the poppies and tulips, acting as a gentle echo and creating weight in an arrangement that may otherwise feel too flimsy, tying the entire ensemble together.

Resting in the rustic compote, this arrangement is a celebration of color, texture, and the beauty of nature's finest moments. With each element echoing the other, the composition becomes more than just a collection of flowers; it's a harmonious symphony of blossoms, inviting the observer into a world of serenity and wonder.

WEEK 9

Echoing the charm of bygone eras, the white, antique milk glass chalice hearkens back to a time when beauty and elegance were cherished—yet they fit within defined, tidy boundaries. This vintage vessel, with its gentle milky hue, cradles the arrangement, evoking the allure of a delicate dessert. Once, such compact and structured designs epitomized sophistication. The duo recalls an age when meticulous order was admired, a period marked by precise coiffures and societal expectations—yet we've infused a modern touch by steering clear of overt rigidity.

At first glance, the blush, linette mums captivate with their voluminous charm, reminiscent of the softest cotton clouds. Their fluffy blooms, so full and inviting, lay a foundation of gentle coziness. The shadow created by their many overlapping petals creates a depth that is much needed in an arrangement this compact.

The lavender sweet peas, with their graceful tendrils, introduce a subtle wash of color. Their gentle allure tempts the viewer to lean closer, captivated by their delicate fragrance, or perhaps imagining a taste of their exquisite beauty.

The peachy butterfly ranunculus lend their own brand of magic. With petals like wings, they flutter amidst the ensemble, introducing playful dynamism. These blooms,

with their ethereal appearance, seem to be caught midflight, dancing joyfully on the outer edges.

Amidst this bouquet, the concertina irises bridge together the peaches and blushes with the purple of the sweet peas. Their tufted lavender beards beautifully align the softer tones of the arrangement with the bolder purple, like a masterful brushstroke on a canvas. The Sahara sunset spray roses, with their layers of petals rolling over on themselves, heighten the dessert-like appeal of the arrangement.

The inclusion of *Eriostemon* introduces a delightful contrast. Glossy leaves break the potential monotony of softness, adding a touch of texture, while their unopened buds echo the arrangement's soft palette.

This arrangement is a dance of structure and spontaneity, reminding us that beauty isn't always sprawling or grand. Sometimes, it's tucked away in the subtle, intimate details, revealing that beneath the veil of order lies a world of lush and indulgent wonder.

WEEK 10

Embracing the timeless beauty of nature's most neutral shades, this arrangement is a harmonious blend of white and green, evoking purity and tranquility. It is housed in a rustic wooden tray whose modest depth might deceive the onlooker. But with the clever use of floral foam, this design breaks free from its confines, reaching upward with grace and ambition.

The long-blooming spirea branches act as the canvas, their extended form inviting the eye to travel the vertical expanse, hinting at a meadow stretching endlessly toward the horizon. These branches possess a naturally curving lilt that should be not only embraced but accentuated whenever possible. In the world of flowers, many blooms have had their very nature stripped away in breeding. Flowers with strong scents tend to die faster, so scent is bred out in favor of longevity. Twisting stems are bred to be straighter to make them fit neatly into boxes for shipping or to make them easier to process. Finding and using elements such as this spirea, most likely sourced domestically while in season rather than shipped from overseas, can go a long way toward adding that natural element back into your arrangements. Nestled amidst the spirea are bunches of white lilac, their fragrant blossoms clustered together in a delicious, weighty texture that begs to be palmed like a ripe bunch of grapes.

O'Hara roses grace the scene, their classic petals unfurling in pristine white, but with a secretive, almost blushing heart that lends a hint of warmth. They're a subtle nod to the transformative beauty of nature, mirrored by white majolica spray roses that fill the interior of the arrangement. Their velvety, cream petals, like fresh homemade whipped cream, add to the opulence of this display. The full, dense lusciousness of these blooms adds weight to the design and invites the viewer to grab a spoon or a palette knife and swirl the rich cream around.

The butterfly ranunculus, Ariadne, has been left out for a few days to fade the color. Initially a pale pink, these blooms have mellowed over time, their hues softening from a youthful vibrancy to a matured cream like the perfect vintage silk dress, exemplifying nature's ability to evolve in elegance.

Interspersed throughout is the sterling range, its silvery-green foliage enhancing the serene color palette, offsetting the rich fullness of the center of the arrangement with a sparkly quality. Without this element, the spirea, with all its texture, would feel too out of place and untethered in this composition.

This arrangement is a symphony in texture and movement, a demonstration that sometimes restraint in color can lead to a wealth of luxurious opulence. It celebrates nature's richness and showcases how, even within constraints, beauty can ascend and flourish.

WEEK 11

A h, the peony—an eternal symbol of spring's opulent embrace, holding a special place in the heart of many. This week's arrangement magnificently showcases two exquisite varieties: Sarah Bernhardt (a true pink with flecks of dark pink in the inner petals) and gardenia (where blush-colored outer petals house an even softer pink hue within). Each peony, with its layers of delicate petals, exudes an effortless grandeur, capturing the very essence of nature's luxurious tendencies. The peony is almost always near the top of the list of favorites for flower lovers.

Housed within a tall, narrow vase of dark-green ceramic, the arrangement is accentuated by the vase's unique faceted design. This touch not only adds depth and intrigue but complements the soft folds of the peonies, creating a harmonious visual dance.

From this richly adorned vase, sprigs of jasmine vine emerge, winding their way skyward as well as cascading gracefully down the side and off to the left. Although I did attempt to marry the jasmine into the arrangement while creating drama by cascading it out and down, I must be honest that looking at it now, I feel I missed the mark. The jasmine feels too separate from the rest of the composition. The longest piece needs a friend in the form of a shorter piece to help bridge its way back into the rest of

the arrangement. It also could have done with a mirrored piece up top to balance everything. This was less obvious in person, but it is always important to keep the final purpose of your arrangements in mind.

Adding to the rosy splendor are large pink parrot tulips, their petals mimicking the gentle curve and color of a flamingo's neck, their painterly petals reflecting every shade of pink to bridge them all together cohesively. Pink ranunculus seem to echo the deeper pinks found in the intricate layers of the Sarah Bernhardt peonies. A touch of mauvey pink statice further enriches the palette. Her main purpose is to fill spaces where bare stems would have been noticeable and unattractive, without creating too much weight as to crowd these heavy flowers and weigh the whole composition down.

Anchoring this elevated bouquet is the fresh plum foliage at its base. Its deep purple not only sets a stage but also intensifies the surrounding pink hues, making them pop and drawing the eye inward.

This arrangement is an ode to the peony, and, indeed, to the very spirit of spring itself—a time of renewal, rebirth, and rhapsody. With each element thoughtfully chosen and placed, it invites the observer to take a moment, breathe deeply, and revel in the lavish beauty that nature bestows upon us.

WEEK 12

S et in a rustic stone urn, the arrangement is a vivacious ode to the vibrancy of coral hues. The vivid display is, without a doubt, dominated by the striking Coral Expression roses. With their unmistakably bright color and plush petals, these roses are a testament to nature's flamboyance.

Complementing the Coral Expression, the vibrant pink ranunculus bloom with a radiant glow, their layers of petals unfolding with passion and fervor. Not to be overshadowed, the majestic coral tree peonies unfurl in opulent grandeur, while the coral flowering kalanchoe adds an unexpected botanical touch to the mix, in the form of texture that breaks apart the repetitive shape of the circular flowers dominating the arrangement.

The Queensland tulips, with their blush fringed edges, introduce a delicate softness to the fiery coral ensemble. These tulips, resembling delicate fabrics with their fringe, create a visual appeal that's both tactile and delightful. The Blushing Parasol spray roses are introduced to build harmony between the subtler hue of the tulips and the brightness of everyone else, softening the energetic coral display with their gentle embrace.

Yet, amidst this coral dance, it's the contrasting tones that tie everything together. The chartreuse viburnum flowers burst forth, their bright-green tones serving as

the perfect foil for the dominating coral. The hellebores echo this sentiment, adding little green stars throughout, with their subtle nod to early spring and the reawakening of life.

The overall shape of this arrangement is subtly asymmetrical, with the smallest bit of drama in the form of a low-slung hellebore and an almost imperceptible reach up to the right. In its entirety, this dense and lively arrangement captures the essence of a blooming coral reef, teeming with color and life. Every glance toward it promises a fresh burst of energy and a vivid reminder of nature's relentless passion.

WEEK 13

As the grip of winter's chill starts to loosen in the North, the vibrant blooms of the South eagerly awaken, basking in the sun's warmth. This week's arrangement paints a vivid picture of this merging of seasons and regions, seamlessly intertwining the delicate cherry blossom branches with the robust essence of Southern blooms.

The arrival of cherry blossom season is always cause for anticipation and joy. In an age when globalization and industrialization have made many flowers accessible year-round, cherry blossoms retain their unique temporal charm. Unlike flowers grown in controlled greenhouses, cherry blossoms remain subservient to the whims of Mother Nature, dependent on natural seasonal patterns. Their susceptibility to late winters or early frosts, coupled with their inability to bloom prematurely in greenhouses, makes them all the more treasured. And so, it's vital to showcase these blossoms in their full grandeur; trimming them too much or burying them deep within an arrangement would be nothing short of sacrilege.

From my very own Nashville garden, the Lichfield Angel garden roses take a proud stance. Their creamy petals, unfolding with a gentle elegance, radiate a distinct Southern charm. The blush baptisia, also a gem from my personal garden, has its own whispered allure—each stem a testament to intimate moments in communion with nature. These unindustrialized

stems, with their unique quirks and bends, infuse an element of the unexpected, elevating the arrangement to a work of art. The gentle downward nod of the garden roses or the nonuniform curvature of each baptisia stem—these are the details that create the design.

However, it's the large purple tree peonies that demand attention. With merely three of these majestic blooms, the arrangement radiates an undeniable splendor. The deep purple at their core casts intriguing shadows, and their sheer presence is so dominating that adding more would border on extravagance.

The Globemaster allium, with their structured heads, complement the scene, mingling with the heady scent of the purple lilac. Together, they construct a majestic backdrop, echoing the richness of the season's transition.

Nestling this floral melody is a blue-and-white chinoiserie-style ginger jar. It bestows a touch of classic sophistication, much like the allure of cherry blossoms. With its detailed patterns and timeless design, the jar accentuates the beauty of its floral inhabitants, culminating in a display that sings of the harmonious interplay of evolving seasons and converging climates.

WEEK 14

In a world where fast-paced change is the norm, nature still takes her sweet time, and the results are truly worth the wait. Just like the fleetingly beautiful cherry blossoms, the darkly alluring blooming *Cotinus*, popularly known as the smoke bush, remains an uncultivated gem, its season unwaveringly dictated by the natural rhythms of Mother Earth. As the smoke bush reveals its purplish-red plumes, one can't help but marvel at the raw elegance they exude. In floral design, the hunt for unique materials is always on, and what could be more unique than a flower that looks more like a plume of smoke? Notice how the blooms of the smoke bush are kept to the outer edges. This allows light to pass through them to accentuate their distinctive nature.

Resting upon a regal ceramic column, this ensemble floats majestically, its base—a reusable plastic tray, often termed a Lomey® dish—cleverly hidden with care in the foliage of the smoke bush.

Yet, amidst this lavish setting, the tree peonies once again claim the spotlight. When working in this scale, it's important to include focal flowers that pack a punch in terms of size. The unparalleled heft of these tree peonies makes them an automatic choice for anchoring such a grand display. It's not merely their size that adds weight, but the story they carry. Each tree peony plant undergoes years of maturation before revealing its blossoms, making every petal a chapter of dedication and growth. These blooms are not just flowers; they are artifacts of nature's unhurried artistry, symbols of the time and commitment required to bring something truly special into the world. A more cost-effective alternative to tree peonies could be hydrangeas. Yet another way to create the right amount of weight for a large branch arrangement is to group together larger-scale flowers like roses.

Adding depth to this luxurious tableau are sprigs of red astilbe, their feathery spikes painting an image of a sylvan wonderland. Meanwhile, the dusty-pink garden spray roses introduce a gentle romance, their clustered petals a soft counterpoint to the more dramatic elements. And then, just when you think the masterpiece is complete, hints of blush phlox emerge, lightening the arrangement's deeper tones, like sunbeams breaking through a twilight canopy.

In this composition, each element not only contributes its unique beauty but also echoes the profound stories of nature's pace, persistence, and perfection. It's a reminder that some of the most beautiful things in life cannot be rushed, and true artistry takes time.

WEEK 15

Nestled within a contemporary cylindrical terra-cotta pot, this week's arrangement unfurls and billows outward, its contents brimming to three times the vessel's size, a signature of my personal style. This design choice tends to communicate abundance and lush luxury. It's an eloquent testament to nature's ability to be both bountiful and nuanced in the same breath.

Serving as the arrangement's foundation is the golden blooming smoke bush. Its blooms, a symphony of blush and verdant green tones, present a delicate dance of color and texture, mirrored by its foliage in golden green. These intricate shades set the stage for the pièce de résistance: the Pastel Elegance peonies. Their soft pastel-peach hues, ranging from slightly darker to a faded brilliance, depending on their stage of bloom, are breathtaking. And while their name, "Pastel Elegance," hints at their rare and sublime beauty, one must be cautious not to confuse them with "Pastelegance." The former, a hybrid peony, is smaller than the tree form of the latter. I have only found this particular variety once, for this very arrangement. However, this look can be achieved with Coral Charm peonies if you allow the blooms to age a bit and fade in color.

Accentuating this lush canvas are heuchera leaves, freshly plucked from the garden. Commercial florists rarely employ these, given their short stems and propensity to wilt away from water; they are not typically sold commercially. However, these fun plants are easy to find at gardening stores and nurseries, as they are an oft-used plant for landscaping. They come in many colors, often referred to colloquially as coral bells. Their rarity in arrangements only adds to their allure, emphasizing a connection to nature and a gardener's approach to floral design. Aptly named "caramel," this particular variety is infused with a unique texture and color that can't be pinned down to any specific hue, changing color depending on its position and the light.

What is most enchanting about this arrangement is its intricate color play. No single hue dominates. Instead, the viewer is treated to a shifting palette of greens, golds, peaches, and the faintest brushstrokes of pink. It's a masterpiece of subtlety, an ode to the complex simplicity of nature. Each component carries within it a spectrum of hues, making the arrangement not just a visual treat but a study in the delicate complexities of nature's palette. This assembly is as much about texture as it is about color—fluffy, rich, and layered, it beckons the viewer to lose themselves in its depths, discovering new details with every gaze, despite only having three elements.

WEEK 16

Perched atop a small antiqued glass chalice, this week's arrangement feels almost like an opulent paradox. Its grandeur and volume, juxtaposed against the delicate stature of the vessel, create a visual reminiscent of a chic diva, draped in a lavish, oversized fur coat, balancing gracefully on slender stiletto heels.

The star of this luxurious ensemble is, once again, the tree peony, resplendent in its coral hues. Its petals spread out generously in some places and remain subtly closed in others, making a statement that's both bold and elegant. Setting the stage for this regal bloom is the Mary Milton viburnum. Unlike its more common green and white counterparts, this variety is distinctive, characterized by its darker, almost brown-tinged leaves and clusters of blush flowers. The blush on these flowers is not typical either. It's dappled and nonuniform, adding to its uniqueness and lending that ethereal quality of "natural" that I'm always seeking in my arrangements.

Mirroring the elongated elegance of the Mary Milton viburnum are the long, softly curving stems of blush baptisia. Their length extends, drawing the eye outward and creating a reaching effect, echoing the creep of nature when left to its own devices.

Rounding off this sophisticated display is the heuchera leaf named "Ginger Ale." At a glance, it presents a sunlit golden green on its upper surface, but a closer inspection reveals a secret: a deep fuchsia underside. This unexpected burst of color masterfully weaves together the various pink and green shades sprinkled throughout the arrangement, bringing cohesion and a touch of whimsy to the piece. Heucheras are not typically sold in the cut-flower world, but these plants are easy to find at a local nursery and come in an unbelievable array of colors. In my experiments with using them as cut elements in arrangements, I have found that cutting in the early morning and giving them a period of rest in cold water is helpful in promoting their longevity. If you have a cooler, definitely give them a bit of time in the cooler before using. With the right harvesting techniques, heucheras can supply a vast array of options for a splash of unexpected color.

Together, these elements converge to paint a picture of timeless elegance with a hint of modern flair—a testament to the beauty that emerges when the past and present intertwine.

WEEK 17

rranged within a tall, cylindrical cut-glass vase, this week's arrangement captures the essence of that moment between spring and summer and its eclectic beauty. The vase, reminiscent of a sparkling hurricane candle holder, casts refracted light that complements the burst of color while obscuring the messiness of the stems within, painting a scene that dances between the lines of opulence and simplicity. Due to the transparent nature of the glass, a tape grid is the best technique for this arrangement.

At its foundation, the vining honeysuckle doesn't just lie subdued. Instead, some tendrils reach out, cascading upward and outward, playfully defying the oval shape of the arrangement. These organic contours impart a wild, untamed charm, reminiscent of nature's capricious spirit.

It's the Coral Charm peonies that truly command attention. These stunning blooms, showcased in various stages of openness, tell a visual story of transformation. The brightest coral hues gently mature into a soft, delicate pink as the peonies age, a metamorphosis that evokes a sense of fleeting beauty and the constant ebb and flow of life.

Diverging from the simplicity of previous weeks, this arrangement boasts a delightful mélange of blossoms. The two-toned pink-and-white ranunculus add playfulness with their intricate, bubblegum-pink petals, while the peachy garden spray roses infuse a touch of muted warmth.

But perhaps the most unanticipated star in this botanical tapestry is the godetia. Often ignored at the wholesaler due to its unassuming buds, godetia unfolds much like a multiheaded, smaller sibling of the poppy when given time. The bright pink-and-white blooms of this variety emerge with an understated elegance, and for a price much less prohibitive than its poppy counterpart. Godetia comes in an array of lovely colors, many of which are two-toned.

In all its diversity and vibrancy, this week's arrangement celebrates the lesser known, the transformational, and the constantly evolving dance of nature. It stands as a testament to the idea that beauty often lies in the journey, in the act of blooming, and in the ever-changing hues of existence.

WEEK 18

Evoking a sense of timeless grace, this week's arrangement unfurls from a blue-and-white chinoiserie vase, a piece reminiscent of age-old artistry. In its embrace, the carefully chosen florals and greens stand in poetic contrast, creating a tableau that feels as much like a remnant of history as it is a fresh burst of nature.

With baptisia foliage laying a foundation, the design takes flight—both literally and figuratively—with the ethereal white stems of campanula. These linear blooms, dotted with their signature bell-shaped heads, dance upward and to the left, choreographing a ballet of blossoms in the air.

As if nature itself is painting a canvas, white sweet pea vines cascade gracefully, invoking drama. Their subtle drapery serves as a counterpoint to the campanula's upward trajectory, crafting a symphony of complementary directions and dimensions. This downward curve of the sweet peas portrays an impression of lavishness, suggesting that the sheer weight of the abundant blooms is causing them to elegantly sag. Yet, the magic lies in the illusion; if the other blooms genuinely weighed down on the vines, the arrangement would appear compressed, losing its intended impact. This careful balance ensures that the design retains its airy charm and dynamism.

Amidst this symphonic spread of whites, the "gardenia" peonies emerge as the debutantes of the ensemble. Their soft blush tones infuse the arrangement with warmth, each petal resembling a puff of cloud softly tinged by the evening sun. The fullness and fluffiness of these blooms command attention, drawing eyes and hearts alike and contributing to the feeling of overabundance and indulgence.

To the right, adding a touch of mystique and intrigue, is the phlox. This isn't just any phlox, but a unique variety that tells a story of history and elegance. Although I'm relatively sure it's a new variety, of which I don't even know the name, it has an antique quality that fits the classic appeal of peonies, sweet peas, and campanula. Its creamy hue, reminiscent of antique lace, is accented with strokes of purple, as if each petal were hand-painted by an artisan of yore. This intricate play of colors acts as a subtle crescendo in an otherwise serene landscape. Adding layers of depth and wonder, this phlox variety exudes an old-world charm.

The entire ensemble, with its cascading sweet pea vines and billowing campanula, evokes the serenity and timeless beauty of a classic English garden. Resting within the iconic chinoiserie vase, the arrangement bridges the elegance of traditional aesthetics with the vibrancy of fresh blooms, creating a display that whispers tales of yesteryears and classic beauty.

WEEK 19

In a world where contemporary design meets the wild, untamed beauty of the garden, this week's arrangement emerges as a testament to the delicate balance between modernity and timeless nature. It is housed in a chic white ceramic vase, distinguished by its tripod stance, painted with blue flecks. This composition boasts an elegantly ovoid silhouette. Its shape subtly follows an asymmetrical S-curve, cascading from the top left and drawing the eye gracefully to the lower right, encapsulating the dynamic between order and organic spontaneity. This shape is one I often use for centerpieces and console tables.

The heart of this arrangement beats with the vivid Dr. Alexander Fleming peonies, which light up the scene in a burst of vibrant pink. Their brilliance is gently tempered by large garden roses in dual shades of peach, with each bloom interweaving and harmonizing with the next, crafting a visual symphony. These roses and peonies, both garden classics, carry the weight and soul of the composition, grounding it with their lush presence.

Gently hovering above, like whispers of a spring breeze, are the lavender sweet peas. Their gentle dance mimics the flit of a butterfly's wings, staying close to the core yet teasingly fleeting. The arrangement gains a touch of further whimsy with the bright-pink *Saponaria* playfully

darting around its edges. I literally refer to elements such as these as "butterflies" when designing. Sometimes a stiff and lifeless arrangement can be instantly revived by adding these "butterflies" in at the end.

Yet, it's a singular pansy that captivates the eye and heart in a manner most unexpected. While design principles often caution against lone elements in mixed compositions, this pansy, plucked from my garden, and having hybridized from two separate pansies I planted, effortlessly proves the exception. With its two-toned, almost tie-dyed allure, it creates a bridge between the muted garden roses and ethereal lavender sweet peas, standing as a gentle reminder that sometimes, in art as in life, the rules are meant to be bent, if not broken.

Navigating the delicate balance of a "colorful" palette is a dance of sophistication and subtlety. The challenge lies in merging multiple hues without overwhelming the senses or veering into visual cacophony. This arrangement triumphs in this endeavor, weaving together colors with mindful consideration of tone and saturation. A frequent pitfall in crafting colorful ensembles is the overuse of similar tones across different hues, resulting in a display that can be visually exhausting. By juxtaposing bright, vivacious colors with softer, muted shades, the arrangement avoids this trap, achieving a harmonious balance that is lively yet soothing to the eye. The vibrant Dr. Alexander Fleming peonies, for instance, harmonize with the subtler shades of garden roses, creating a dynamic dance without descending into chaos.

WEEK 20

One of my favorites from this project because of its simplicity and elegance, this week's arrangement showcases the beauty and potential of locally sourced flora. With only three ingredients, it's a masterclass in minimalist yet striking design. It serves as a gentle reminder that sometimes, less truly is more, especially when the ingredients chosen shine with a distinct brilliance.

The foundation of this exquisite composition is the captivating buddleia variety Silver Fountain. This isn't your typical shrub. Its long, sweeping branches laden with small lavender flowers reach skyward before cascading gracefully, almost water-like, down to touch the table and even spill over its edges in an embrace. The drama of this delicate cascade serves as an enthralling spectacle, drawing eyes and souls into its dance.

Nestled amidst this fountain of buddleia is the vivacious purple campanula. Its local sourcing, a testament to sustainable and close-to-home flower farming, ensures it stands tall, full, and resilient, embodying the kind of natural vigor that can often be lost in global shipping. The bouncy stems inject height into the arrangement, allowing the cascade of buddleia to flow around it.

Now enters the surprise star: the humble petunia. A darling of grandma gardeners everywhere but often

overlooked in bouquets, it's reborn in this context. I fell in love with this particular variety after seeing it in my mother-in-law's garden (grandmas really do have a wealth of knowledge for mining) and deciding I needed it in my own garden. I'm always testing things in my garden for vase life, and these petunias astounded me with their longevity. Not many flowers live for a full two weeks after cutting. Stripped from its usual surroundings and given the spotlight, it's almost transformed, so different that it might just prompt a double take. Its appeal is not just about its deep purple core, which seamlessly ties it to the other elements, but its pale, almost ethereal faces that bring a splash of light to the arrangement's heart. Beyond its beauty, the petunia's journey here serves as a commentary on the global flower industry, highlighting how commercialization can sometimes obscure nature's treasures.

Cradling this trio of wonders is a large ceramic vase, gourd shaped and glazed in a teal green that complements the floral hues while grounding the arrangement. It's an embodiment of nature's synergy and the art of floral design, reminding us that when we look closer to home, treasures often await, ready to surprise and enchant.

WEEK 21

This week we venture further into the profound beauty of minimalism, where less really becomes more. Here, the gentle pink cosmos takes center stage, not by being opulent or grand, but through its simple elegance, multiplied by the art of repetition.

As if plucked from a serene countryside meadow, the cosmos radiate a soft, childlike joy with their sunny yellow centers. Arranged in variances of height, they showcase their tender faces and gracefully arcing stems. Each cosmos seems to dance to its own rhythm, with some nodding gracefully and others reaching skyward. It's a choreography of nature, with every movement deliberate, every curve considered.

The set of nine mint-colored bud vases, all echoing the same soft hue but varying in voluptuous form, further amplifies this dance. Each vase, reminiscent of a gourd with its undulating curves, plays its part in the display. They are carefully staggered, adding depth to the composition, ensuring the eyes meander through the arrangement, appreciating every individual vase and flower, yet never losing sight of the collective beauty.

This design strikes a fine balance, and that's its hallmark. The ratio of visible flower to vase is meticulously maintained. If one were to envision the entire arrangement framed within a pair of rectangles stacked atop each other, the vases would nestle perfectly within the lower rectangle, their tops marking its boundary. Meanwhile, the upper rectangle would be graced with the soft pink petals of the cosmos and their slender stems, each reaching out, yet contained predominantly within this boundary. Just a whisper of flowers would dare to stretch beyond, breaking the perfect horizontal line, introducing a delightful spontaneity that prevents the composition from appearing too rigid. This precise vase-to-flower ratio is a design choice that helps to create visual harmony and rein in what could verge into chaos. Every stem, whether curving downward or looking up, is given its moment, its space. This isn't just an arrangement; it's a visual symphony. The minimal foliage on the cosmos, only a hint of their frilly leaves, ensures the essence of the flower isn't lost in a crowd.

What's remarkable about this week's piece is its whispering power. In its hush tones and delicate placements, it commands attention, proving that sometimes simplicity, when orchestrated with intent and vision, can be the loudest statement of all. And it's just so happy!

WEEK 22

Nestled within a slender, rectangular vase is a decadent bouquet that feels like a secret garden encapsulated. These are not your typical roses; they emanate a sense of old-world charm, reminiscent of those roses one might stumble upon in the tucked-away corners of an English countryside garden.

Each bloom is delicate, with layers upon layers of petals that seem to whisper tales of nature's intricate design. These garden roses have a freedom to them, a wildness. Their slender stems allow their heads to naturally bow and nod, creating an enchanting dance of flowers that appear to be engaged in a delicate ballet of nature.

The arrangement plays on depth and dimension: roses are artfully nestled deeper within the bouquet, while others are coaxed forward, as if reaching out for a soft touch. This clever placement gives the impression of the roses being lovingly stacked atop one another, an ode to opulence and abundance.

Colorwise, the bouquet is a subtle symphony. Dominated by creams and blushes, there are whispers of soft orange, peach, and tender pink that flow seamlessly. However, the yellow roses, strategically placed, act as the silent conductors of this floral orchestra. One graces

the upper right peak, while its counterpart mirrors its radiance lower and to the left, subtly guiding one's gaze through the arrangement and ensuring harmony and balance in this seemingly spontaneous composition.

In its entirety, this arrangement captures the very essence of a garden in full bloom, with roses cascading over one another, each telling its own story, yet beautifully synchronized in a dance of colors, depth, and form.

WEEK 23

As if capturing a majestic scene straight out of the heart of summer, this arrangement reaches skyward, evoking an almost palpable warmth and vibrancy. Held within a statuesque, smoky glass cylinder, its grandeur is immediately striking. One can't help but be reminded of the spontaneous beauty one might glimpse on the side of the highway during a sun-soaked summer road trip: the kind of untamed nature that flourishes, unnoticed, as vehicles speed by.

The hollyhocks, in their sultry, nearly black blooms, serve as a rich backdrop, contrasting against the brilliant sun-kissed appeal of the ProCut Plum sunflowers. These sunflowers, unique in their coloring and disposition, hold a commanding presence in the center and toward the right, their petals reflecting the hues of a late-summer sunset. Grouping them together creates a focal point for the eye, a needed resting place in a very textural and wild composition.

Balancing this dominance, the graceful arches of golden ninebark and the towering hollyhocks stretch out assertively to the left, as if swaying with a gentle summer breeze. The large green thistles contribute an element of earthiness and rugged beauty, while the various grasses intersperse soft, cloudlike plumes throughout, giving an

ethereal touch to the composition, in the same way that a cloud of grasses swaying in the breeze along the side of the road does. The oak leaf hydrangea foliage, with its autumnal reddish-brown leaves, grounds the design, subtly hinting at the transition from the peak of summer to the gentle embrace of fall. This assembly not only showcases the splendor of the season but also the artistry of combining textures, colors, and forms in a harmonious yet dramatic tableau.

WEEK 24

Nestled within an aged terra-cotta compote, encrusted gently with nature's own tapestry of green moss, lies an arrangement that beckons with a gentle summer serenade. The base, composed of scented geranium foliage, sets an immediate tone of refreshing earthiness. The curly leaves draw parallels to the lush vibrancy of freshly picked summer vegetables and verdant leafy greens.

Central to this botanical tableau are three varieties of dahlias. With each dahlia bearing a distinct hue, shape, and size, they span a harmonious palette of purples, uniting in their role as the arrangement's focal point. But the true artistry in working with dahlias lies not just in their selection but in their positioning. Though they often present with straight-facing, broad fronts, the key to their integration is to resist forcing them to face outward. When constrained to a singular direction, they can flatten the depth and dynamism of the arrangement. But when allowed their natural inclinations—sideways, tilted this way or that, or even facing downward—they contribute a multidimensionality to the overall composition. It's a dance of respect, where their organic tendencies can either make or break a design. The secret lies in embracing their authentic selves, letting them flow and settle as they naturally would.

Complementing this royal hue, the Japanese anemones grace the arrangement with their tender lilac petals, the darker purple undersides purposefully revealed for a nuanced depth. Their buds, a rich dusty purple, bob playfully at the top of the arrangement like little pollinators. Delicately interwoven among these primary blooms is a rarer variety of cosmos, dappled with soft lavender and hints of sunlit yellow at its core. The star-shaped summer clematis drift toward the edges, creating an ethereal border with their light-purple faces. And as a finishing touch, the pink snowberries introduce a fresh texture and grounding heft, their spherical forms punctuating the display with a delightful contrast.

Though replete with diverse elements, the arrangement maintains an elegant cohesiveness. It adopts an oval form, the breadth overshadowing its height, casting an expansive embrace that captures the spirit and hues of a perfect summer twilight.

WEEK 25

This week's composition draws inspiration from an object that marries both artistry and functionality: an aged terra-cotta vessel sculpted in the visage of a woman. Her soft expression becomes the foundation upon which a tapestry of blooms is woven, both eclectic and classical.

At the heart of this composition are dahlias once again. Dahlias tend to enchant with their unique character and wide variety of shapes and shades, so when they're in season they must be used as often as possible. The larger variety immediately captures attention with its generous, sun-drenched petals, predominantly yellow but marred with streaks and flecks of red. So meticulously scattered are these blemishes that one might mistake them for an artist's deliberate brushstrokes, yet nature is the true painter here. Joining them, a second variety of dahlia presents a dance of dual tones: a soft hue of orange graces the front of its petals, while a richer, deeper shade tints the backs. As mentioned earlier, when working with dahlias it is paramount to remember their inherent desire for freedom. Their beauty is amplified when they are allowed to orient themselves naturally, whether sideways, downward, outward, or inward; embracing their authentic tendencies lends depth and dynamism to the ensemble.

Complementing the dahlias' vivid palette are zinnias that seem to have been plucked straight from a '70s canvas. Their burnt-orange and mustard-yellow tones evoke a retro charm, adding layers of nostalgia and warmth. Interspersed among these florals are the expansive helecho ferns, their sprawling fronds lending a verdant contrast. These ferns play a crucial role, ensuring balance from left to right and front to back, their placement artfully asymmetrical, fostering a sense of organic movement while balancing the shape of the composition.

As a finishing flourish, explosion grass dances amidst the arrangement, its tiny sprigs reminiscent of distant stars or celebratory confetti, introducing an element of whimsy and texture. The collective, from vessel to verdure, tells a story that is at once ancient and utterly in the moment, a testament to the art of juxtaposition and harmony.

WEEK 26

Housed in a vintage footed vase made of green glass is an arrangement that pays tribute to one of the summer's most splendid offerings: dahlias. With their fleeting presence each season, it's only apt that they take the spotlight once more. And this week, it's all about celebrating them in hues of pink.

At the core of this arrangement, we have four distinct varieties of pink dahlias. The "Café au Lait" dahlia, always a crowd favorite, lends its creamy blush hues, harmonizing beautifully with the intense pop of the large, hot-pink, semicactus dahlia that confidently claims its space in the composition. Bringing in delightful nuances, the "Strawberries and Cream" variety enthralls with its soft blush petals, adorned with streaks of a more pronounced pink. This careful play of light and dark pink subtly ties the different shades together. Additionally, a vibrant hot-pink ball dahlia, its specific name unknown, rounds out the dahlia showcase, adding another layer of texture and color.

Accompanying our dahlias, we have the pink phlox (which boasts no less than three shades of pink, if examined carefully) and blush garden roses, their delicate tones seamlessly blending with the theme. The Double Alissa

Champagne lisianthus introduces a graceful elegance, its frilly petals adding a softness that is different than that seen in the dahlias. To wrap it all up, strands of green hanging *Amaranthus* cascade from the arrangement, offering a lush, chartreuse contrast, giving the entire piece a feeling of dripping in floral abundance. The result? A harmonious ode to pink dahlias in all their multihued glory.

WEEK 27

E choing the theme from Week 21 (page 101), this week's arrangement embraces a similar sense of minimalism and repetition, but with a twist to suit the evolving seasons. Set in a series of gourd-shaped vases, now cast in a stark, elegant black, the arrangement paints a serene picture of late summer transitioning to fall.

Instead of the lively pink cosmos, this week highlights the subdued beauty of various grasses and pods. Their elongated forms and subtle hues encapsulate the essence of a waning summer. The neutral tones and gentle sway of the grasses reflect the tranquil, muted energy that the end of summer brings, while the pods offer a nod to the promise of the upcoming season's harvest.

Among the standout inclusions is the explosion grass. With its effervescent seed heads, it imparts an almost sparkly illusion, akin to a sky dotted with distant stars. This particular grass not only adds texture but introduces an element of lighthearted whimsy, seeming to twinkle with every soft movement. Complementing this ethereal presence is the ruby red silk grass. It cascades gracefully, arching out of the vase in a manner reminiscent of a water fountain, bringing with it a fluid dynamism and an evocative sense of motion.

As with the previous ensemble, the positioning is key. The grasses, varying in height and volume, are artfully arranged to create an ebb and flow of visual interest. Their delicate tops sway and lean, just as nature intended. Some pods are placed in such a manner that they nestle close to the vase's mouth, while others jut out slightly, adding depth and dimension.

This series of vases, in their deep black hue, offers a stark contrast against the softness of the grasses, emphasizing the fleeting beauty of summer's end and the anticipation of fall's embrace. The simplicity, repetition, and choice of materials evoke a sense of peace, a quiet reflection on the changing rhythms of nature.

WEEK 28

The centerpiece of this week's arrangement is a striking vintage brass vessel, sculpted in the exquisite form of a nautilus shell. Its spiraled elegance is amplified by the cascade of flowers emerging as though a tide brought them to its open end. Assisting in this artful display is a ball of chicken wire placed inside the shell, helping to hold the stems securely while allowing them to take on their natural forms.

Dahlias, our recurring summer favorite, take center stage once more. In shades of vibrant coral, they immediately evoke images of sea urchins, their intricate petals mirroring the delicate spines and layers of their oceanic counterparts. Their presence in this nautical-themed vessel strengthens the connection to the deep blue sea. Take note of how one of the dahlias is partially obscuring another in a layering effect. This is a perfect example of how to create depth in your arrangements by pushing some stems in and pulling others forward.

Further exemplifying the marine theme are the decorative leaves and flowers of some begonias cut from houseplants. In soft coral and pure white, these blossoms hang down, almost appearing like sea anemones swaying with the currents. Their accompanying leaves serve as a

cozy nest for the dahlias, providing a lush backdrop and enhancing their vibrant colors.

Adding a touch of whimsy to the arrangement is the scabiosa "Fata Morgana." With their pompon-like structures, they seem to frolic and hover just above the overall composition, like playful sea creatures dancing in the sunlight.

Together, all of these elements combine to transport the observer to an underwater world, turning a simple floral arrangement into a deep-sea exploration.

WEEK 29

There's an undeniable radiance to this week's floral offering. Cradling the strikingly large white blooms of the cosmos is a vintage ceramic vase, painted in a sunny yellow that, upon closer inspection, seems to be a tribute to the very centers of the cosmos themselves. The vase, a Mod-era treasure, is slick to the touch, with a glaze that gives it a gloss echoing days gone by.

The cosmos chosen for this arrangement hail from the "Cupcakes White" variety. Their name aptly hints at their uncanny resemblance to white cupcake papers, a playful nod to both nature's mimicry and human creativity. Layer upon layer of these captivating blooms fill the vase, creating a feeling of fullness and abundance. Amongst the profusion, a solitary cosmos stands slightly aloof, its face gracefully tilted toward any hint of light, symbolizing nature's inherent quest for growth.

To achieve the precise arrangement, it is imperative to use a tight tape grid. This technique (using the vase tape discussed on page 20) ensures each stem finds its place without feeling constrained. It's worth noting the importance of foliage management in this design. While the lacy green leaves of the cosmos are undeniably beautiful, they can also distract and overcrowd. By thoughtfully removing the majority, the essence of the design is retained

without allowing the arrangement to become overly busy. However, a sprinkling of these leaves remains, reminding the observer that flowers and their foliage are partners in the dance of nature.

A word on positioning: due to the natural bell-like posture of the cosmos, these flowers display best from a slightly elevated perspective. Placed atop a shelf or mantel, their bowed heads become a spectacle, revealing the intricate details often missed in a traditional setting.

WEEK 30

Summer is in its zenith, just before the temperatures start to fall, and what better way to pay homage to its splendor than with an arrangement that sings with warmth, vibrancy, and celebration? Week 30's arrangement is a radiant testament to the season, spotlighting the beloved Free Spirit rose at its core.

The Free Spirit rose is a legend in its own right. Favored by many for its unique interplay of colors, this rose truly embodies the passionate dance of summer. Each bloom is generously sized, unfurling beautifully to reveal petals that cascade gently, creating a graceful ruffle. At first glance, the rose captivates with its intense orange hue. But upon closer inspection, delicate nuances of pink start to emerge, hinting at its versatile nature. Not just a feast for the eyes, the Free Spirit rose also indulges the senses with its classic rose fragrance, adding another layer of luxury to the arrangement.

Accompanying this iconic rose is the humble marigold, a flower that resonates with sunny days and beaming smiles. Its deep orange tones flawlessly accentuate the center of the Free Spirit rose, creating a harmonious bridge of color. Complementing this are the tender petals of the Blushing Parasol spray rose. These blooms, with their soft pink hues, mirror and emphasize the pink guard

petals of the Free Spirit, adding depth and dimension to the palette.

But the surprises don't end there. Enter the cockscomb celosia, a true summer wonder. With its form reminiscent of underwater coral, it introduces a texture that's both unique and delightful. Its vibrant shades—spanning the entire spectrum from the deepest oranges to the softest pinks—create a rich tapestry that ties the entire arrangement together.

To conclude, the pink eucalyptus flowers make their mark. They're not your everyday inclusion, but their unusual texture and playful form add a touch of the unexpected, a whimsical nod to summer's penchant for fun and spontaneity.

In essence, Week 30 is not just an arrangement; it's an ode to summer, capturing its heat, its joy, and its unbridled spirit in every carefully chosen bloom.

WEEK 31

Set within the vivid scenery of a traditional Mexican hand-painted vase accompanied by matching candlesticks, this arrangement feels like a poetic ode to Mexico's rich horticultural legacy. The soft yellow ball dahlias, which are indigenous to Mexico, anchor the composition with their bold and tightly packed petals. These are harmoniously accented by buttery yellow zinnias, giving a sunny warmth to the arrangement. The Aztec mix zinnias, with their mesmerizing transitions of brown, yellow, and red, infuse an earthy depth, paying homage to ancient Mexican civilizations.

There's an unexpected but delightful twist with the inclusion of fresh basil and tomato vines. Their aromatic presence hints at a Mexican kitchen garden, and together with the chocolate lace, they bring layers of texture and a sense of flourishing abundance.

Finally, the fresh dates on their stems cascade from the arrangement like nature's own jewelry. Their dual tones—some still a verdant green, while others show a glimpse of ripening yellow—symbolize the transition of time, from the youthful summer to the more mature autumn.

This arrangement is a feast for the senses—it captures not just visual beauty but also evokes scents and flavors, reminiscent of a sun-soaked Mexican countryside.

WEEK 32

As the curtain begins to close on dahlia season, it's fitting that we dedicate this week to celebrating the marvelous versatility and spectrum of this flower. Housed in an arrangement that seems to capture the essence of a sunset, we journey through the myriad hues of pinks, oranges, and yellows, and every sublime shade that dances in between.

The unique beauty of the dahlia lies not only in its color range but also in its diverse classifications. From the intricate spikiness of the cactus variety to the soft, dreamy layers of the water lily; from the robust and round ball form to the delicate petals of both the formal and informal types, and the singular beauty of the anemone dahlia—this composition showcases them all. The blueberry foliage acts as a delicate backdrop, making the radiant colors pop even more.

Designing with just dahlias is an exercise in balance and intuition. They're a testament to the idea that while similarity offers cohesion, it's diversity within that similarity that delivers dynamism. The key is to let each dahlia express its individual character. Forcing them to all face forward strips away their charm and leads to a two-dimensional look. Instead, embrace their idiosyncrasies.

Allow their faces to turn, tilt, and bow in varied directions, capturing light and shadow differently. As you place them, push some deeper into the arrangement while allowing others to hover just on the surface or even soar slightly above. This dance of depth breathes life into the composition, ensuring a multidimensional, vivacious display that is nothing short of breathtaking.

WEEK 33

As we edge toward the end of summer's warmth, a transitional elegance permeates this week's arrangement, echoing the whispers of the upcoming harvest season. Mums, with their traditional autumnal feel, combine with the trailing grandeur of *Amaranthus* and the season's last grapes, painting a picture of abundance and change.

The structural asymmetry of this piece is striking, characterized by an elegant upward and rightward sweep. The sky-reaching heights and slender, towerlike structure of blue delphinium, the nascent promise of lisianthus buds, and the prickly appeal of tall blue eryngium create a sense of stretching toward the last rays of summer sunshine. Adding to this vertical exuberance are the dusty blush trails of *Amaranthus* and the petite, round allure of Jewels of Opar.

Grounding this airy composition are the more solid forms in the bottom quadrant. Moab roses offer a full-bodied opulence, while dusty linette mums bring the feel of incoming cooler days. The blush lisianthus provides a bridge between the towering heights and the arrangement's base, its gentle color echoing the heights of *Amaranthus* above. A particularly delightful touch is the stem of grapes, bifurcated in its ripening journey, with half of its bulbs a deep, luscious purple and the other half still bathed in the green of earlier days. These grapes cascade just so, as if lazily resting after a summer of growth, their tips brushing against the table.

Blue tweedia sprinkles its delicate charm throughout, ensuring the rich blue tones of the delphinium are echoed and balanced. And finally, anchoring this entire tableau is a rex begonia leaf, borrowed from a houseplant. Its broad surface and rich texture offer both a visual and thematic grounding, tying together the season's last hurrah with the promise of what's to come.

WEEK 34

In this week's composition, we pay homage to the powerful allure of understated elegance and the juxtaposition of dark and delicate tones. The arrangement is rooted in a vintage trophy cup crafted from deep-black glass, an embodiment of solemnity and reverence.

Acting as a natural extension of this somber vessel, dark stems of ninebark rise upward, particularly concentrated on the left side, creating an impression of shadows dancing in moonlight. Amidst this mysterious setting, the blush lisianthus, with its open centers revealing an unexpected deep black, emerges as the star. Each lisianthus bloom, gracefully poised on a slender stem, imparts movement and an ephemeral beauty. As these stems sway and bend, they become an integral part of the visual narrative, a testament to the idea that every element, no matter how unassuming, contributes significantly to the whole. A concentration of lisianthus blooms in the center works to create a whole that gives the piece some visual weight, grounding it.

While the blush lisianthus offers delicate femininity, the blush upright *Amaranthus* and rose hips interject a touch of autumn's richness. These elements, however, do not detract from the central theme; instead, they gently reinforce it by echoing the pink tones of the lisianthus.

However, the unsung hero of this tableau is undoubtedly the jewels of opar. Despite their diminutive size, these tiny buds create an impact that's hard to overlook. Scattered throughout like confetti thrown in a soft breeze, they add layers of depth and interest, proving that sometimes it's the smallest details that leave the most indelible mark.

WEEK 35

The waning warmth of summer converging with the embrace of fall is truly a sight to behold. It's during these moments that nature commingles its colors, textures, and scents, offering a kaleidoscope of inspiration for the discerning eye.

Nestled within a rustic cast-iron urn, our arrangement for this week serves as a reflection of this vibrant transition. The wild and dramatic *Diervilla*, foraged from the untamed outdoors, establishes itself as the anchor. Its year-round brownish-red leaves, evocative of autumn's signature palette, stretch defiantly beyond the floral perimeter, invoking an organic, unrestrained allure.

Central to the ensemble are the deep-burgundy formal dahlias. Their bold and sophisticated presence is elegantly juxtaposed with the delicate "Café au Lait" salpiglossis. This harmonious pairing is further accentuated by the yellow pincushion centers of the anemone dahlia. To infuse brightness amidst this rich canvas, deep-pink dahlias are interspersed, casting their luminous glow. The evolving shades of the viburnum berries, gradating gracefully from verdant green to warm oranges and deep reds, narrate a story of nature in flux.

This arrangement is more than just a gathering of flowers and foliage; it's a celebration of the season's transitional spirit. It serves as a vivid reminder that inspiration often lies in the everyday, in the nature that surrounds us. The incorporation of foraged diervilla is a testament to the idea that beauty often exists in the overlooked, in the corners of our world we pass by daily.

Taking a moment to truly see and appreciate these elements can lead to creations as enchanting as this week's piece.

WEEK 36

The allure of hydrangeas has always been their size, but for the antique variety, it lies in their intricate dappled coloring, reminiscent of masterpieces by Impressionist painters. Their soft, watercolor-like hues of blue, purple, green, and pink create an ethereal spectacle, like a canvas come to life.

For this week's arrangement, set within a classical terra-cotta urn, these blossoms take center stage. The urn's aged patina and stately design contrast beautifully with the fresh vibrancy of the blooms. A crucial pro tip when working with terra-cotta: always line it with a waterproof liner (discussed on page 20), like the papier-mâché one I've used. This ensures the longevity of your arrangement and safeguards against any potential damage to surfaces.

Hydrangeas, despite their enchanting beauty, pose a unique challenge. Their rounded, consistent shape can often lead to a lackluster arrangement if not handled with intention. When creating a design using just this variety, it's essential to reimagine their potential. This involves breaking away from the ordinary and embracing a layered, textured approach.

With a collection of around 30 stems, spanning four distinct varieties, the arrangement seeks to redefine hydrangea aesthetics. By extending some blooms beyond

the central cluster and angling others for a cascading effect, a more dynamic visual story unfolds. Some blooms serve as supporting characters, subtly concealed, laying the foundation for depth and volume. It takes a bit of courage to render some blooms almost invisible, but that courage is necessary and rewarded within the finished product. A sprinkling of foliage plays its role too, accentuating the layers and enhancing the 3D effect.

The success of this design lies in meticulous placement and the artful juxtaposition of the hydrangeas' varied hues. By leveraging their inherent gradations of color, you can sculpt light and shadow, adding depth, movement, and intrigue to the composition. It's an ode to nature's paintbrush, a symphony of shades and structures, and an exercise in turning uniformity into a unique, evocative spectacle.

WEEK 37

The ancient Chinese long honored the four noble plants, each symbolizing a unique virtue. The chrysanthemum, representing vitality and longevity, was celebrated not only in folklore and festivals but also in art and decor. In our antique Chinese vase, hand-painted chrysanthemum blossoms unfurl in detailed splendor, setting the scene for this week's arrangement.

The vase, with its intricate botanical depiction, demands an equally captivating composition. The early pink pampas grass, in its prime glossy phase before it matures into feathery fluffs, rises majestically, coupled with the plum foliage that hints at the changing season with its evolving hue. This tall and dramatic backdrop not only complements the vase's grandeur but also counterbalances its form, ensuring the arrangement doesn't appear stunted or dwarfed by the vessel it's contained in.

Chrysanthemums, or mums, as they are fondly called, are the heart of this composition. It's easy to dismiss them based on their commonplace, commercial variants seen ubiquitously. Yet, delve deeper into the world of mums, especially heirloom varieties, and a treasure trove of beauty and diversity awaits. They possess an elegance, charm, and depth that go beyond the generic, challenging our perception and reminding us of their noble lineage.

Their history, intricacies, and cultural significance in Chinese traditions are encapsulated in their delicate petals.

Adding another layer of intrigue are the large purple artichokes, whose architectural form offers a fascinating contrast to the softer textures. The vibrant red ruby silk grass, cascading gracefully from the vase's mouth, provides the arrangement with a finishing touch of drama and movement. The burgundy tones of the plum, grass, and artichokes bring the colors of the painted vase up into the arrangement itself.

Working with such a large and ornate container challenges the designer to think big, and not just in size, but in symbolism, history, and sentiment. It's a harmonious blend of cultural reverence and modern interpretation, where the age-old appreciation of the chrysanthemum meets contemporary floral design techniques.

WEEK 38

Autumn, a season often painted with broad, fiery strokes in popular culture, is, in truth, a nuanced symphony of changing hues. The vibrant and varied spectacle of the Chinese pistachio branches epitomizes the understated beauty of this season. These branches, from a singular tree, possess a duality that mirrors the transition of summer to fall: while the deep-red branch anchors the arrangement's left, the green-yellow-brown one on the right presents an evolving narrative, painting a story of gradual transformation.

The red coleus, snipped just before autumn's chill could claim it, adds richness and depth to the composition. It's as if each leaf, with its veined intricacies, is a testament to summer's last stand. Nestled amidst this foliage are the final trio of "Café au Lait" dahlias from the garden. Their delicate petals capture the essence of fleeting beauty, offering both a melancholic farewell to summer and a warm embrace to the cooler months.

Complementing these dahlias are the creamy peach garden spray roses and the equally creamy terra-cotta spray carnations. Their subtle hues not only bridge the dramatic contrast of the pistachio branches but also introduce a softness to the arrangement. The upward sweep of broom corn grass, perched on the top right, is perfectly juxtaposed with the gentle droop of the deep-pink snowberry on the left, creating a dynamic yet harmonious balance.

Peppered within this rich tapestry of fall colors is the surprising and delightful presence of purple cleomes. Their unexpected inclusion breaks the mold of traditional autumnal arrangements, proving that nature, in its infinite wisdom, always has a wild card up its sleeve.

This arrangement is a celebration of fall's subtle spectrum, an ode to its quiet transformations, and a gentle reminder that change, while inevitable, can be breathtakingly beautiful.

WEEK 39

In the spirit of All Hallows' Eve, this arrangement taps into the mystical aura of Halloween, blending traditional elements with unexpected twists. Crafted in a moss-draped terra-cotta urn, its classical form immediately conjures feelings of time past, of tales whispered through the ages. But it's the contents of this urn that truly mesmerize.

With the entire composition crafted from preserved elements, this arrangement promises longevity, a timeless ode to the eeriest of holidays. The foundation is made of the ethereal baby eucalyptus, whose preserved form retains all its intricate beauty. Treated with dyes to achieve muted autumnal tones, the dusty purples and burnt oranges elicit a sense of mystery, reminiscent of a fading sunset on an October evening.

The dried purple artichokes, majestic in their rich hue, anchor the arrangement. Their unique form, evoking ancient flora from another realm, captures immediate attention. These artichokes act as the still heart of this creation, surrounded by the undulating dance of the eucalyptus.

Emerging from this autumnal sea are the contorted filbert branches. Twisting and meandering, they reach upward as if touched by an otherworldly force.

Their barren, gnarled form stands in stark contrast to the softness of the eucalyptus, adding a touch of the macabre.

Yet, this arrangement isn't just confined within its vessel. Like the tendrils of a haunting tale, elements of the design spill onto the table, with eucalyptus and another dried artichoke lying in wait. These elements break the boundary between the vessel and its environment, suggesting that the magic within is not easily contained and making it a perfect entry-table display for the holiday.

And for those with a keen eye, a surprise awaits. Tiny skulls, hidden among the flora, peer out with hollow gazes. A subtle nod to the theme, they are guardians of this enchanted garden, a quiet reminder of the fleeting boundary between life and death.

Evoking the rich tapestry of Halloween lore, this arrangement is both a tribute to the season and a testament to the power of nature, preserved in time, to tell a story that transcends the ages.

WEEK 40

Enveloped in the rustic embrace of a terra-cotta compote, this arrangement beckons the observer with the subtle charms of autumn's allure. As if painted by nature's own brush, it encapsulates the transitioning canvas of the season, telling a story of change, endurance, and beauty.

At the rear, dogwood branches artistically extend, evoking a gentle ballet of nature. The duality of their coloration—with the right side donning a deeper hue of red, while the left flirts with green and a mere kiss of red—creates a captivating backdrop. It's as though time has paused in this very moment, capturing the transition from summer's lushness to autumn's fiery passion.

The arrangement then invites you closer with a cascade of creamy salmon-pink carnations. These flowers, meticulously stacked, form a linear pathway that guides the eye from the base to the pinnacle of the arrangement. Their delicate hues and ruffled texture give them a soft, dreamy quality, contrasting with the boldness of the dogwood.

However, it's the golden-toned roses that truly steal the show. Full and opulent, their guard petals hint at a touch of burgundy, resonating with the deeper shades of

the dogwood. These roses stand as guardians, anchoring the design with their regal presence.

For a touch of whimsy and movement, the blush upright *Amaranthus* and broom corn grass seamlessly intermingle. Their delicate strands dance and sway, adding dynamism and texture to the composition. They whisper tales of meadows kissed by the first frosts and of winds carrying the scents of ripe fruits and woodsmoke.

Finally, the gold-tinted, almost metallic heads of the *Banksia* ser. *Dryandra* serve as nature's own jewelry, capturing and reflecting the light and adding unexpected luminosity to the ensemble.

Every element in this arrangement harmoniously coexists, bringing forth an ode to the delicate balance of the season. It's a reflection of autumn's inherent duality: the warmth of its colors juxtaposed against the coolness of its breeze, and the nostalgia of an ending juxtaposed against the promise of rebirth.

WEEK 41

D renched in the lustrous hue of turquoise, the glazed vase instantly commands attention, demanding an equally lively congregation of florals and foliage. This week's arrangement captures the spirit of autumn while breaking away from traditional, muted tones—opting instead for a jubilant palette reminiscent of a vivid sunset.

Like the flames of a roaring fire, the turning maple leaves set the sky aflame in this ensemble, reaching upward, bold and unapologetic. They symbolize autumn's finale: the crescendo before the calmness of winter.

Tenderly accompanying the maples are the viburnum berries, poised at that magical interim between orange and red. Their transitional hue adds a delightful dimension, reinforcing the concept of change and progression. The viburnum, in its duality, further diversifies the composition. While some stems gallantly rise, others gracefully cascade over the vase's edge, painting a picture of balance and harmony.

Dahlias are artfully interspersed. The soaring yellow water lily dahlias contribute both height and brilliance. Their robust petals capture the sunlight, radiating an almost ethereal glow. Positioned more intimately are the buttery orange-yellow dahlias, which meld seamlessly with the cherished "Peaches 'n' Cream" variety. Together, they narrate a tale of warmth and comfort.

Serving as nature's own mosaic are the ranunculus blooms. Each petal is a marvel, holding within it a spectrum of autumnal shades. Their intricate detailing and delicate disposition provide a beautiful contrast to the boldness of the other elements.

However, it's the green persimmons that infuse a touch of whimsy. Dangling from branches, they seem like nature's own ornaments. The few that lie gracefully at the vase's base ground the arrangement, connecting it to the earth from which all its components sprang.

This arrangement is a celebration, a fiesta of fall that embraces the season's vibrancy while looking forward with hope and anticipation to the wonders that lie ahead.

WEEK 42

T ucked in an almost poetic embrace, the snowberry foliage lays the foundation for this week's tableau. Not conventionally celebrated for its foliage, this variety of snowberry redefines convention, enchanting with stems that curve gracefully like ballet dancers midpirouette. The cold has painted them in a tender mosaic of soft oranges and yellows, allowing the petite clusters of pink berries to shine through like distant stars on a dusk canvas.

But it is amidst this gentle backdrop that the majestic white garden roses rise, asserting their regality. Their ample, cupped forms lend a gravity to the composition, acting as serene islands in a sea of dynamic foliage.

Yet, as is often the case, the dahlia refuses to be overshadowed. This water lily variant unfurls its petals to reveal the resplendent hues of an autumn sunset: radiant pinks, fiery oranges, and soft, sunlit yellows. It's as if the horizon itself has lent its most heartwarming shades to these blossoms.

The butterfly ranunculus, in their delightful nectarine hue, seem almost serendipitous. A mirror to the dahlia's grandeur, they amplify the peach undertones of the snowberry foliage, ensuring it doesn't go unnoticed.

Acting as the harmonious bridge between stark contrasts, the butter-yellow ranunculus eloquently connects

the creamy purity of the roses to the multicolored spectacle surrounding them. This gradient of color is enhanced by the golden nandina berries, which are shyly peeking out, still clinging to their golden hue before the inevitable transformation to bright red.

The arrangement is finally crowned by sprigs of grapevines, their leaves slightly bronzed as if kissed by the early frosts. Their inclusion is a nod to the cycle of nature, the continuity of seasons, and the fleeting beauty of the moment.

In its entirety, this arrangement doesn't just replicate the beauty of fall—it sings its symphony, full of soft melodies and passionate crescendos, a dance of nature in all its twilight glory.

WEEK 43

Crafted in an elongated wooden trough, this arrangement feels like nature's poignant curtain call—a powerful, final burst of autumn's glory just as Thanksgiving beckons. As we gather to offer thanks, this creation mirrors the season, reflecting a culmination of life's bounty and the impending embrace of winter.

Warm-hued dahlias, the stalwarts of autumn, intertwine with the enduring rudbeckia and the statuesque upright *Amaranthus*. Their presence seems almost defiant, reminiscent of fleeting moments filled with sun's mellow warmth now giving way to shorter, cooler days.

The scented geraniums, with their leafy splendor, recall early autumn days, soon to be overpowered by winter's chill. The final transformation of maple branches, swaying in hues of burgundy and green, whisper tales of a season nearing its close.

Glistening among the foliage, viburnum berries in varying shades of orange look like droplets of a setting sun. Creamy mums and taupe carnations, in their muted elegance, anchor the vibrant colors, reminding us of the rich textures and flavors that Thanksgiving brings.

Though spread wide to grace a mantelpiece, this design also elegantly rises, with its crescendo on the left, echoing the fading notes of fall. The arching rudbeckia

stems, turned just so, seem to bow in reverence, honoring the passing season.

As families come together to express gratitude and to feast, this week's arrangement stands as a testament to autumn's fleeting beauty. Just as Thanksgiving traditionally marks the pivot from fall to winter, this display is a heart-stirring adieu to a season's resilient splendor and a gentle welcome to the frosty wonders that lie ahead.

WEEK 44

As the chill of winter deepens, wrapping the landscape in its icy embrace, the floral industry displays an indomitable spirit, drawing upon a vast repository of year-round blossoms. This resilience defies the traditional seasonality that nature has prescribed, showcasing the wonders of global transportation and advanced farming techniques. Flowers, such as the timeless rose, which aren't bound by specific seasons, consistently grace our living spaces, ensuring that nature's artistry remains with us even during the coldest, bleakest winter days. Creating the feeling of winter while using spring and summer flowers is a fun creative challenge.

This week's arrangement offers a glimpse into a winter wonderland, all within the confines of a large, crystal footed vase. This vase, reminiscent of icicles and frozen lakes, sets the perfect stage. Wild, foraged juniper, with its spontaneous growth patterns and distinct aroma, serves as the foundation. Its boughs meander gracefully, some drooping downward like snow-laden branches, while others reach skyward, echoing the patterns of frost-kissed limbs in the wintry outdoors. It's a testament to nature's raw beauty that farm-grown variants simply cannot mimic the innate charm of wild juniper.

Taking center stage amidst this juniper backdrop are the creamy white spray roses, going by the romantic moniker "white majolica." These roses, with their intricate petals, are tenderly embraced by the silvery metallic leaves of rex begonia. The begonia leaves, with their natural luster, not only cradle the roses but also find a home near the base, offering an almost moonlit contrast. Due to their succinct stems, meticulous care is given to ensure they remain hydrated, often resorting to water picks in such a voluminous display. Weaving their way through this arrangement are delicate fronds of white astilbe, the starlike allure of *Astrantia*, and the pristine presence of white statice, each adding intricate layers of depth and texture.

Such a blend of snowy blooms, the icy undertones of juniper, and the metallic gleam of begonia constructs a picturesque winter tableau. As we journey deeper into December, and the warmth of autumn becomes a distant memory, this bouquet stands as a testament to nature's undying elegance and the charming allure of the impending festive season.

WEEK 45

The festive season unfurls its magic, ushering in an era of splendor and joy. In tribute to this enchanting time, this week's arrangement dances in tones of gold and silver, like moonlight on a frosty evening. Presented in an elegant, classic urn, the arrangement is a testament to the holidays' shimmer and brilliance.

The base of this display boasts the lustrous southern magnolia foliage, an evergreen emblematic of Christmas wreaths and resplendent garlands. Interspersed amongst the magnolia is the silvery pearl acacia foliage. Its dainty seed heads glisten like miniature icicles, conjuring images of delicate strands of tinsel or silver beads draped on a tree.

Acting as beacons of purity and elegance, large white garden roses find their way throughout the arrangement. They are in harmonious company with the rare and captivating gold roses, which echo the theme of festivity. White alstroemeria lends volume, serving as a lush backdrop, while the ethereal white *Astrantia*, with its starry blooms, sprinkles a touch of whimsy and wonder.

Elevating the luxe factor, a few stems of preserved baby eucalyptus, painted in a resplendent metallic gold, are gracefully positioned. Their presence, though minimal, is intentional, ensuring the arrangement doesn't

lean into the overtly ornate. These gilded stems find resonance with the gold undertones on the reverse of the magnolia leaves and the few prized gold roses. Ensuring the arrangement remains rooted in nature's authentic beauty, a quaint cluster of pine cones serenely rests at the urn's base.

This composition, with its delicate balance of natural beauty and festive flair, embodies the spirit of the holidays—a season of wonder, warmth, and golden moments.

WEEK 46

As the year draws to a close and the world is enveloped in the serene silence of winter, this week's arrangement stands as a beacon of the promise of new beginnings, echoing both the purity of the new year and the stark, crystalline beauty of winter's depth. Presented in a sleek white ceramic compote, the composition is an ode to the art of preservation and the transformative power of bleaching.

Two majestic palm fans, now rendered in a haunting shade of bone white, anchor the arrangement, their broad fronds jutting gracefully outward in an embracing gesture. The fern leaves, often admired for their intricate, lacelike patterns, take on a newfound significance when bleached. Their feathery tendrils seem to shimmer, each vein standing out in stark relief, underscoring nature's architectural brilliance.

The center draws attention with the bleached poppy pods that then burst outward like shooting stars. A testament to nature's cyclical design, these pods, typically known for their earthy bluish-green hue during the summer, are now transformed into ghostly white specters, evoking an otherworldly allure.

Intermingled with the commanding presence of these main elements are the finer details: the pearl-white spikes of bleached ruscus, the delicate ruffles of bougainvillea, the intricate patterns of white strawflower, and the wispy plumes of bleached bunny grass. The arrangement is softened by tufts of pampas grass, teased from larger plumes and strategically placed to offer a gentle contrast to the sharper textures.

In its entirety, this arrangement is a symphony of white—a myriad of shades, tones, and textures, all harmonizing to create a breathtaking vision. It challenges the viewer's perception of the natural world, showcasing how even in the most familiar elements, there lies a potential for rebirth and reinvention. Ethereal in its beauty and unexpected in its design, it stands as a fitting tribute to the hope and freshness of the year ahead.

WEEK 47

In the heart of winter, when the days seem endlessly cold and the sparkle of the holiday season becomes a cherished memory, it's natural to yearn for warmth and the gentle touch of sunshine. As landscapes lie dormant under frosty blankets, the verdant splendor of tropical locales beckons, promising respite and a dash of exotic allure. And for those who immerse themselves in the world of florals, this longing can be somewhat satiated through the magic of tropical foliage.

This week's arrangement is a passport to those distant, sun-drenched shores. Crafted in a moss-covered compote that conjures images of grand stone urns gracing the entrance of opulent estates nestled amidst palm trees, it's an ode to the lushness of the tropics. Monstera leaves, iconic in their shape, serve as a sturdy backdrop, evoking the dense jungles and rainforests where nature thrives in its untamed glory.

Foxtail ferns, with their feathery, arching fronds, add a sense of movement, reminiscent of gentle sea breezes rustling through coastal groves. The trailing asparagus plumosa fern, with its fine, needlelike leaves, delicately skirts the arrangement's perimeter, bringing a softness that contrasts beautifully with the bolder elements.

Taking center stage is the elegant umbrella fern, its slender stems and dainty leaflets cascading forward like a waterfall. Amidst this verdant tableau, gardenia foliage introduces bulk, grounding the arrangement with its glossy leaves, while a stray tendril of philodendron, with its heart-shaped leaves, spills over one side, adding a touch of wildness.

The Calathea leaves, with their striking white stripes, provide a visual break from the sea of green. Their patterns, reminiscent of nature's own artistry, introduce an element of intrigue, capturing the mystique of tropical nights.

In creating this arrangement, there's not just a celebration of nature's luxury but also an acknowledgment of the transportive power of floristry. Even as winter persists, with this verdant display, one can momentarily step into a world where the air is warm, the nights are alive with the sounds of chirping cicadas, and the promise of spring doesn't seem quite so distant.

WEEK 48

Following on from last week's tropical escapade, we continue to find solace in our verdant hideaway from winter's grasp. The southern hemisphere, with its warm embrace, offers a captivating contrast to our chilly surroundings. Our journey this week brings us to the confines of a simple green glass vase, reminiscent of recycled or sea glass.

At the foundation lies the lustrous green gardenia foliage. Rather than imposing a rigid structure, some of these verdant leaves are allowed to recline naturally, setting an organic tone for the unfolding tableau.

Yet, amidst this greenery, the undisputed protagonist of our arrangement is the anthurium. Its appearance is nothing short of bewitching; an enigma of colors—a blend of pinks, taupes, peaches, and even muted flesh tones—dances on its surface. Its spadix stands tall, starting in a muted green and gradually transforming into a creamy almond beige, harmoniously echoed by the spathe that surrounds it.

Synchronicity in nature is a marvel, and this is epitomized by a unique variety of *Leucadendron* sourced from the Australian landscape. Its top leaves, in a shade of almond beige with the faintest blush of pink, mirror the anthurium's palette almost uncannily. Discovering such

harmonizing elements in the vast world of flora is akin to unearthing hidden treasure, reinforcing the belief that sometimes, the most serendipitous finds are those not actively sought-after.

Anthuriums, much like dahlias, possess a certain whimsical quality. Rather than reining in this free spirit, each bloom is allowed to dictate its own dance within the vase. Turning and pivoting, they build layers of movement and depth, crafting a tableau that's a testament to nature's unpredictability and unmatched artistry.

WEEK 49

As the frosty tendrils of winter continue to grip the world outside, the wonders of greenhouse-grown flowers transport us into a world where spring is in full bloom. This week's assemblage is beautifully showcased in a vintage pink cut-glass candy dish, reminiscent of bygone eras when such dishes held sweet treasures.

Foliage is conspicuously absent in this masterpiece; it's a celebration of blossoms in all their glory. The foundation of this bouquet is set with billowy lavender stock, exuding a fragrance that's enchanting to the senses. Some liken its aroma to cloves, while others, including myself, find it reminiscent of the nostalgic scent of Necco wafers. On its own, stock can effortlessly stand as a centerpiece, but in this tableau, it serves as a prelude to an even grander display.

Acting as the heart of the composition are the David Austin Keira roses, chosen deliberately in a state of near bloom. Their tender pink cores resonate beautifully with the hues found in the year-round snapdragons, gifts from Canadian greenhouses. Anemones, with their blush-kissed undersides, further accentuate this pink symphony.

Adding depth and a touch of drama are the regal, deep-purple anemones. Their intensity is harmoniously balanced by muted purple carnations and the whimsical

streaks and speckles on the alstroemeria. This intricate dance of colors and fragrances creates a pathway, leading us right back to the comforting embrace of the lavender stock.

Indeed, this arrangement is a declaration of spring's promise, an optical illusion so convincing that it makes one almost believe that winter's reign has come to an end.

WEEK 50

Stepping into this week, I present an ode to the oft-underestimated carnation. Elegantly perched within an antique silver chalice, this piece seeks to redefine the way we perceive these commonplace blooms. It stands as a testament to the belief that every flower holds within it the potential to inspire awe, provided we approach it with intent, vision, and a dash of innovation.

Brought to life using the Moon series of patented carnation varieties by Florigene, the hues on display range from the softest lavender to the deepest, richest purple. There's an inherent harmony in the choice of three distinct tones; each plays its part in this choreography of color.

Echoing the structural dynamics of the hydrangea composition from Week 35 (page 149), this creation thrives on contrast and depth. Asymmetry, rather than detracting from its beauty, adds to the allure. By positioning some blossoms deeper within the shadows of the chalice and allowing others to reach boldly outward, a visual dance emerges. The varying tones of purple, each representing a different beat in this ballet of blooms, further accentuate this effect, playing with light and shadow, drawing the eye and captivating the heart.

Yet amidst this sea of purple, one stem stands out—a unique, gray carnation kissed with the faintest hint of purple. A beautiful anomaly, possibly the result of a rare genetic variation, this singular stem serves as the centerpiece. Its striking difference from its counterparts only adds to its allure, demanding attention and further cementing the idea that with vision and creativity, every flower, regardless of its commonality, has the potential to inspire wonder.

In this piece, the humble carnation rises, shedding any preconceived notions and firmly taking its place as the star of the show, illustrating that with imagination and craft, even the most familiar can be transformed into the extraordinary.

WEEK 51

As winter's grasp wanes, the international flower trade brings a prelude to spring from Europe's blossoming fields right into the hands of florists in the United States. This week, we dive deep into the grandeur and grace of these fresh arrivals.

Nestled within a tall, slender stone urn, a meticulously designed garden is sculpted. It's a balanced blend of nature's wildness and a florist's deliberate touch, offering a sneak peek into the spring yet to bloom in full. Draping gently, baby eucalyptus forms the initial canvas, setting forth a soft and romantic color palette that dances between delicate blush and pristine white.

In this gathering of spring's finest, it's a delightful challenge to discern the true showstopper. Is it the pale anemones, boasting an arresting black heart, or perhaps the barely blush ranunculus, flaunting countless immaculately layered petals? Take note that ranunculus of this size do well with a bit of fortification via a wire. Check the Commonly Used Tools and Mechanics section of this book (page 19) for more details on that. Adding depth to the arrangement, the deep-pink *Astrantia* and butterfly ranunculus intermingle, contrasting beautifully with the lighter shades. The hellebore, a herald of imminent spring, is present, nodding its beautiful head amongst the other blooms.

Even with all that, there's more! Feathered blush astilbe lends a touch of unique texture, while snapdragons effortlessly bridge the hues of gentle blush and profound pink. Then, subtly stealing the scene, are the sweet peas. Bathed in the faintest blush, their delicate tendrils carry an enchanting aroma that stands unmatched in the floral world. Their ethereal ruffles, both dainty and spellbinding, echo sentiments previously shared in this book; the sweet pea, in all its fragility and charm, imbues any arrangement with a magic that's truly incomparable.

WEEK 52

As winter gracefully bows out, spring emerges, unfurling its delicate beauty, bringing the seasonal cycle full circle. This concluding arrangement of our year-long journey pays tribute to spring's early whispers, capturing its subtle romance in the midst of an otherwise austere landscape.

Setting the visual and textural stage for this botanical ballet are the nascent plum branches. Emerging from their dormant state, they reach outward, their leaves not yet fully unfurled, symbolizing nature's perennial hope and renewal. These branches, with their untamed vigor, are reminiscent of spring's own tentative steps, painting a backdrop of deep-burgundy anticipation.

Yet, amidst this backdrop, the undisputed protagonist is a singular rose: the Moab. This recent addition to my bouquet of favorites stands out, not just for its aesthetic charm, but for its sheer grandiosity. Many roses of standard varieties offer a restrained bloom, opening only slightly until they eventually wilt. But the Moab? It dares to be different. Echoing the multifaceted hues of the Moab Desert, this rose is a harmonious confluence of brown, taupe, and pink. With every passing day, the Moab unfurls further, becoming an ever-expanding canvas of layered petals.

Originally, my vision for this week's arrangement encompassed a diverse medley of flowers. However, as I began the creative process, it became abundantly clear that nothing I added could match the intrinsic beauty the Moab rose brought to the tableau. Respecting its undeniable charm, I allowed it to dominate the composition. The focus shifted from diversity to playing with nuances—the interplay of light, shadow, and form. The careful positioning of each Moab, turned to catch the light just so, brought forward the intricate details of its spiraling petals.

The end result is akin to a visual sonnet. A cascade of Moab roses, each at its most full state of bloom, creates a dynamic sea of petals. They shimmer, reflect, and absorb light, presenting a breathtaking vista that captures the very essence of winter's quiet romance.

CONCLUSION

As we reach the end of this floral journey, it's my hope that *Everyday Bouquet* has brought a touch of nature's beauty into your space, no matter the season. The world of flowers is vast, vibrant, and ever-changing, and this collection represents just a snapshot of that wonder.

The cycle of seasons is a reminder of nature's rhythms and the beauty inherent in each phase of life. By tuning in to this cycle, we deepen our connection to the world around us, finding joy in the details and fostering appreciation for the transient beauty that flowers bring.

The art of floral design is much more than just placing flowers together; it is a delicate dance of form, color, space, and texture. Each arrangement we've explored throughout this book has served as a testament to the transformative power of thoughtful design. Rooted in foundational principles such as the importance of space, the play of colors, the rhythm of repetition, and the enchantment of variety, we've journeyed through a world where flowers tell stories, evoke emotions, and create atmospheres.

The Free Spirit rose arrangement of Week 30 (page 132), for instance, encapsulates the essence of what we've learned. It's not just about the rose itself, but how it interacts with the marigold's fiery hue, the delicate pink of the Blushing Parasol spray rose, and the unexpected texture of the pink eucalyptus flowers. Such combinations exemplify the importance of looking beyond the individual flower to the larger picture, the whole story that an arrangement narrates.

Our forays into color bridging illuminated the subtleties in how hues interplay and affect our perception. By understanding and harnessing these intricacies, a floral designer can conjure contrast, emphasis, and feelings of harmony, even leading the viewer's eye on a deliberate journey across an arrangement.

Moreover, as we delved into the significance of negative space, we came to appreciate the beauty in the unseen, the unoccupied. These voids are as critical as the flowers themselves, providing balance, enhancing focus, and allowing each element to breathe and shine.

The principle of repetition reminds us that there's a rhythm in design, an underlying beat that the human brain finds innately satisfying. And yet, variety keeps that rhythm fresh and

unpredictable, ensuring that our designs always have an element of surprise and delight.

Beyond these principles, what stands out is the heart and soul of the designer. The very acts of foraging, choosing each stem, and placing it with intentionality give life to a piece. Each arrangement is not just a static display but a living, breathing entity that evolves, resonates, and communicates.

As we conclude this exploration into the world of floral design, it's worth noting that while principles and guidelines are foundational, the true magic lies in the designer's personal touch, their connection with nature, and the stories they wish to tell. Every flower has a story, and so does every arrangement. It is our privilege and joy as designers to be the storytellers, crafting tales of beauty, emotion, and wonder for all to experience.

Here's to the endless journey of discovery, creativity, and the sheer joy of floral design.

ABOUT THE AUTHOR

Most people attribute their floral passions to family members with green thumbs. However, **ALEX VAUGHAN** was an apartment-raised child born in Miami. She found inspiration not through a gardening family, but in her father's bustling boat workshop, absorbing the art of mechanics and the intricacies of entrepreneurship.

It was in a quaint flower shop on Newbury Street in Boston where her true floral passion ignited. There, she discovered the enchanting world of peonies and experienced the magic of spring for the first time, and decided to dedicate herself to the world of flowers.

Her journey continued in Los Angeles, where she explored various floral styles while working in multiple flower shops. Along the way, she met her future husband, and together, they moved to New York City. While she refined her floral craft there, she yearned for a space to grow her own flowers.

In 2015, Alex founded FLWR in Nashville with her husband Quinn. The city embraced FLWR's unique approach, and their venture quickly became one of Nashville's best. Today, they are transforming three acres into a floral paradise at FLWR, with a mission to source directly from their perennial flower farm.

Her path in the floral world may seem unconventional, but she stands as living proof that one doesn't need a legacy to thrive within this community. Her story inspires others to find beauty in every petal, emphasizing that a genuine love for beauty is all one needs.

To support Alex's continuing floral journey, follow her @flwrshop or visit flwrshop.com.

ABOUT THE PHOTOGRAPHER

NICOLA HARGER is a commercial and editorial photographer based out of Nashville, Tennessee. Known for her way with light and use of negative space, Nicola has a strong instinct for finding moments of discovery and significance in her work. She collaborates with all kinds of brands, studios, and creative agencies across the country to execute campaigns and art-forward projects that express their essence and message with ease. Making beautiful things that speak to people is what she cares about the most. You can see more of her work at nicolaharger.com or find her on socials at @nicolaharger.

Many thanks to Telicia Lee for providing the backdrops used in all of the photographs.

ABOUT CIDER MILL PRESS BOOK PUBLISHERS

Good ideas ripen with time. From seed to harvest, Cider Mill Press brings fine reading, information, and entertainment together between the covers of its creatively crafted books. Our Cider Mill bears fruit twice a year, publishing a new crop of titles each spring and fall.

"Where Good Books Are Ready for Press"
501 Nelson Place
Nashville, Tennessee 37214

cidermillpress.com